# CARD GAMES

THE WORLD'S BEST CARD GAMES

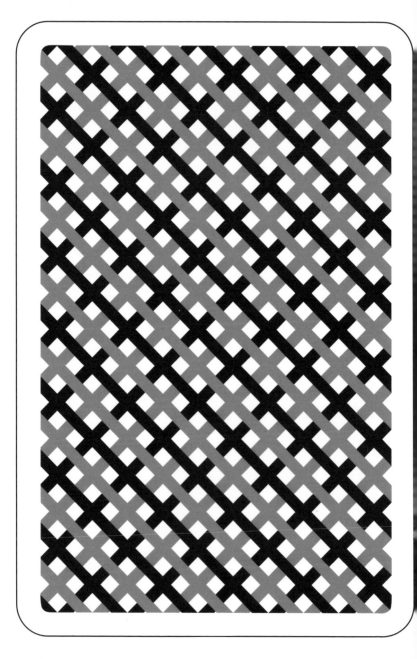

# CARD
# GAMES

## THE WORLD'S BEST CARD GAMES

### SARA HARPER

AMMONITE
**PRESS**

# CONTENTS

# INTRODUCTION

A deck of cards is a very cheap and sociable way to keep your family and friends entertained for hours on end. People have been playing cards the world over for hundreds of years, and there are games suitable for every age group and occasion. One of the great things about card games is that they can be played almost anywhere—at home, while traveling, in a college dorm—so long as you have a deck of cards and a table to play on.

In *Card Games* we've included all the classics—from Authors to Whist, with easy-to-follow instructions and clear illustrations. These popular games range from party favorites like Pig to a few you can play on your own when there's nobody else around. Success in some of these games relies on luck—the cards you are dealt— while others rely on skill, and some need a combination of both.

All the games use a standard deck, or pack, of cards. If you need a piece of paper and a pencil for scoring, or some tokens or counters, this will be indicated in the game instructions. The games are played according to sets of rules, but there are endless variants and there's no reason why

you can't adapt the rules to suit you. The important thing is that everyone agrees on the rules beforehand!

What you play is mainly determined by the age of the players and how many players there are, so the book is organized with games grouped according to age suitability, and each game says how many people are needed to play. Of course, young children might be perfectly capable of learning trickier games, so pick any game you think is suitable.

Card games help children practice math skills, and use memory, strategy, and a whole heap of other tools to outsmart other players. They're great for keeping older brains sharp too. But above all else, playing cards is hugely entertaining—so let's get started!

# HOW TO PLAY CARDS

Read this section before embarking on a game so that you understand the card table conventions of how to choose a dealer, shuffling, the deal, and the direction of play.

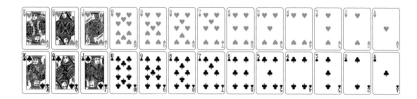

## THE DECK

There are 52 cards in a standard deck, divided into four suits—spades, hearts, clubs, and diamonds—each distinguished by a different symbol. The suits are of equal value except if a particular game says differently.

Each suit contains 13 cards, known as ranks: Ace, 2 (deuce), 3, 4, 5, 6, 7, 8, 9, 10, and the face (picture) cards—Jack, Queen, King. In theory the Ace or one is the lowest card and the King the highest, but in most games the Ace beats the King.

A standard deck usually includes one or more Jokers—most games will require you to remove these. When playing fast, rough games like Slapjack or Snap, old cards are best as a pristine deck will get battered.

## HOW TO CHOOSE THE DEALER

In many games, players cut the cards to choose the first dealer. This involves lifting a section of cards off the top of the deck and showing the bottom card of the section removed. The person with the highest card wins—if there's a tie, the cards are cut again. Or, deal out a card to each player and the one with the highest card becomes the first dealer (deal the cards again if necessary). For the next round of play, the deal passes to the left.

## SHUFFLING

The act of playing cards tends to put them in order, so cards are always shuffled to randomize the deal. If you're new to card games, the easiest way to do this is to place the cards face down on the table and mix them around with your hands before putting the deck

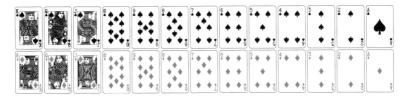

back together again. Experienced players will shuffle overhand by sliding small packets of cards in front and behind each other, or even riffle the corners of two squared-off stacks then release the cards so that they fall interleaved—your cards need to be in good condition to do this otherwise they'll collapse in a dog-eared heap!

## CUT AFTER SHUFFLING BUT BEFORE DEALING

The player to the dealer's left lifts a random number of cards from the top of the deck and then the dealer places the cards beneath on top. The purpose is to hide the former bottom card of the pack as it may have become visible during the shuffle.

## THE DEAL

The dealer deals the cards clockwise, usually one at a time and face down unless otherwise specified. The dealer receives the last card of each round.

## PLAY

Unless otherwise stated, starting with the person on the dealer's left, players take it in turns to put down a card and play is clockwise.

## LEVELS

♠ Simple
♠ ♠ Medium
♠ ♠ ♠ Tricky

# GAMES FOR ALL AGES

Games for all the family can be played by children as young as four or five, right up to older adults. They don't involve much skill but they are a whole heap of fun! Winning is mostly down to luck or quick reactions. Along the way, children will learn about different cards and how to put them in order through matching and sequencing.

# AUTHORS

Also known as Happy Families, the goal in this game is to collect cards of the same value ("rank") where the picture or number is the same. Four cards of the same rank, one from each suit, makes a "book." This game was originally played with a specialty deck but a standard deck of playing cards is just fine.

## WHAT YOU NEED
- Standard deck of cards
- Jokers removed

## DEAL
Any player deals out all the cards, face down and one at a time. It doesn't matter if some players have more cards than others. Players look at their cards and, keeping them hidden from other players, arrange them so that cards of the same rank are next to each other in their hand. This is so that they can see which cards they want to collect.

## PLAY
The player to the dealer's left asks any other player for a specific card, one that matches a card in their hand. For example, if a player has the 10 of clubs, they could say, "John, please give me the 10 of spades." If the person asked has that card, they must hand it over. The player can now ask another person, or the same person, for another rank that matches one in their hand. The player's turn continues until they ask for a card that another player doesn't have, and play then passes to the next person.

Whenever a player collects all four cards of the same rank, they place them face up in a pile on the table in front of themselves. Play continues until all 13 books have been formed, and the player with the most books wins the game.

### STRATEGY
The rules are simple, but pay attention to which cards other players are asking for—they could be trying to make the same book as you. If so, ask them for one of those cards when it's your turn.

Players sort their cards according to rank.
Here, the player should ask another player
for the Jack of diamonds.

An example of a book—a set of four cards
of the same rank.

# BEGGAR MY NEIGHBOR

Also known as Beat Your Neighbor Out of Doors and Strip Jack Naked, this shows children that some cards have special functions, which is a basic concept of many card games. The aim is to win all the cards. If nobody has won after a given time, the person with the fewest cards left is the winner.

## WHAT YOU NEED
- Standard deck of cards
- Jokers removed
- Two decks if more than four players

## DEAL
Any player deals all the cards, face down and one at a time, to each player. It doesn't matter if some players have more cards than others. Players arrange their cards into a neat pile in front of them but do not look at them.

## PLAY
The person on the dealer's left places their top card face up in the middle of the table. The next player places their top card on top of this card. The process continues, each player placing one card on top of the other, until an Ace or a face card is played.

If an Ace or a face card is played, the next player must pay out a number of cards:

**Ace** = four cards
**King** = three cards
**Queen** = two cards
**Jack** = one card

If all the cards put down for payment are numbered (spot) cards, the player of the Ace or face card picks up all the cards from the middle and adds them to the bottom of their pile. That player then turns over their next top card and places it in the middle of the table.

However, if at any point the player paying the penalty turns up an Ace or face card, payment immediately stops and the next player must now pay the penalty instead. This process continues until payment is completed with numbered cards. The game continues until a player has collected all the cards.

Ace or face cards are penalty cards.

PLAYER 1

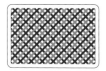

PLAYER 2

Player 1 has played an Ace so player 2 has paid four cards as a penalty. All the penalty cards are spot cards so player 1 picks up all the cards.

PLAYER 3

# CLOCK

Sometimes known as Sundial or Travelers, this solitaire game is very popular because of its unusual layout. You've only a 1 in 13 chance of winning this game, and it's all down to luck—no skill is required beyond the ability to turn over the cards!

## WHAT YOU NEED
- Standard deck of cards
- Jokers removed

## DEAL
Shuffle the cards and deal 13 piles of four cards face down. Arrange 12 piles in a circle to represent the numbers of a clock face with the 13th in the center.

Lay out the cards in the shape of a clock face.

## PLAY
Turn over the top card in the center and place it behind the pile representing its number on the clock—Jacks count as 11 and Queens as 12, other cards their face value. Then play another card from that pile. When a King is turned up it is placed behind the center pile.

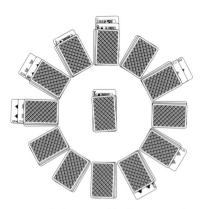

Start with the top card in the center and place it behind the pile representing its number, then play another card from that pile, and so on.

If there are no cards left in a pile, the top card from the next pile in sequence that still has cards is turned over

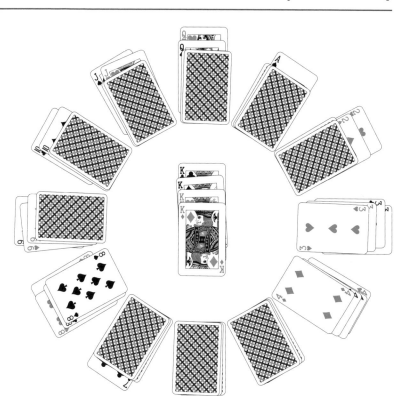

**The game is lost because all four Kings
have been turned over.**

instead. For example, if a 5 is turned over and there are no more 5s left in the five o'clock pile, turn over the top card from the six o'clock pile, or from the next pile that still has cards.

To win the game, you must get all the cards face up. If you turn over the fourth King before all the other cards are face up, you lose because there are no cards in sequence after it.

# GO FISH

A simple game for all ages, similar to Authors (see page 10), the aim is to win the most books, or sets, of cards. A book is any four cards of a kind, such as four Queens, four 5s, and so on.

## WHAT YOU NEED
- Standard deck of cards
- Jokers removed

## DEAL
Any player shuffles the deck and deals out seven cards to each player (five cards for four or more players), one at a time and face down. The rest of the cards are placed face down in a pile on the table to form the stock. Players pick up their cards and, keeping them hidden, sort them into ranks.

## PLAY
The player to the left of the dealer begins by asking any other player for a specific rank that matches one in their hand—for example, "Bonnie, do you have any 8s?" If the person who was asked has any, they must hand them over to the asker. The asker can now ask another player, or the same player, for another card that matches one in their hand, and the player's turn continues.

If the player being asked does not have any of the rank asked for, they say, "Go

A hand sorted according to rank—a player will try to make books with their 3s and 10s.

Two books—four 5s and four Queens.

fish." The player told to fish must draw a card from the stock—if it is of the rank they asked for, they show it to the other players and their turn continues. Otherwise, the next player to the left takes their turn.

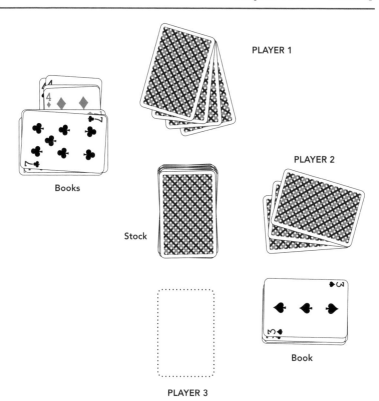

PLAYER 1

PLAYER 2

Books

Stock

Book

PLAYER 3

**Player 3 has run out of cards so may draw
one from the stock when it's their turn.**

During the game, if a player has no cards left, when it's their turn to play they may draw a card from the stock and ask for cards of that rank. If there are no cards left in the stock they are out of the game.

Whenever a player collects all four cards of the same rank, they place them face up in a pile on the table in front of themselves. Play continues until all 13 books have been formed. The player with the most books wins the game.

# MEMORY

Also known as Concentration or Pairs, the goal is to win the most pairs of cards. This game tests a player's ability to memorize card positions, so it's essential that the cards are put back neatly into their rows.

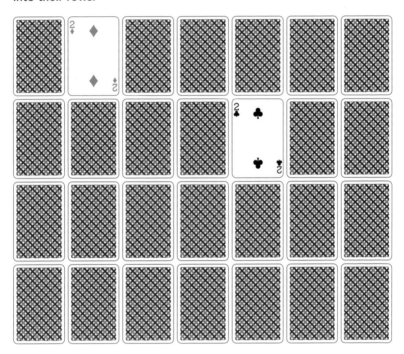

## WHAT YOU NEED
- Standard deck of cards
- Jokers removed

## DEAL
Place the cards face down on the table and move them around to mix them up. Now lay them out neatly in four rows. The youngest player can go first, and then play follows clockwise around the table.

The player has turned up a matching pair,
so can remove them from the layout.

## PLAY

The first player turns up any two cards. If they are of equal value (for example, the 7 of clubs and the 7 of hearts), the player picks up that pair, puts it in front of them, and has another go. If two cards are not a pair, those cards must be placed face down again in the same position. It's then the turn of the next player, and the game continues until there are no more cards left to pick up. The winner is the person with the most pairs of cards.

# MY SHIP SAILS

The aim is to collect seven cards of the same suit, though you can change your mind about which suit to collect as the game progresses. Play is continuous, so instead of taking it in turns to play, the game begins when all players have sorted their hands and are ready.

## WHAT YOU NEED
- Standard deck of cards
- Jokers removed

## DEAL
Any player shuffles the cards and deals seven cards to each player, face down and one at a time.

A player's hand, sorted into suits.

## PLAY
Players look at their cards and sort them into suits. They decide which suit to collect.

Each person puts an unwanted card face down on the table and passes it over to the player on the left, at the same time receiving a card from the player on the right.

Play continues in this way until a player gets seven cards in the same suit. At this point they say, "My ship sails!" and the game is over.

A winning hand, with seven cards all in the same suit.

# OLD MAID

Also known as Pass the Lady, the goal is to avoid being left with the unpaired Queen at the end of the game. Simply remove one of the Queens before you start playing so that one is without a pair.

## WHAT YOU NEED
- Standard deck of cards
- Jokers removed
- One Queen removed

## DEAL
Any player shuffles the cards and deals them all out, one at a time, face down. It doesn't matter if some players have more cards than others.

## PLAY
Players look at their cards and sort them into pairs (two cards with the same number or picture). All matching pairs are placed in a face-up pile in the middle of the table. If a player has three of a kind, they put down a pair and keep the third card until a match can be made later. If a player has four of a kind, they put down two pairs.

The player to the left of the dealer fans out the cards they have left in their hand, face down so that they are still hidden. They offer these cards to the person on their left, who must take one of the cards. If the card matches one the player already holds, they will

discard the pair. If not, they add it to their hand and fan out their cards to offer to the person on their left.

Whenever a player's last card is taken or put down, they drop out. The game continues clockwise around the table until all pairs have been discarded and one player is left holding the old maid. This player is the loser.

PLAYER 1

Discard pile

PLAYER 2

PLAYER 3

Players discard matching pairs of cards into a pile in the middle of the table.

# PIG

This is a super-fun party game that can be played by up to 13 people at one time. The goal is to be the last player left in the game. The cards are all down to luck and there's no skill involved, apart from being quick to react when a player touches their nose!

## WHAT YOU NEED
- Standard deck of cards
- Jokers removed

## CARDS
Any player sorts the cards by rank so that there are 13 sets of cards. You need one set per player so, for example, if there are five players, the dealer chooses five sets of cards and puts the other sets to one side. It doesn't matter which sets are chosen—the aim is to be the first player to collect four of a kind, with no preference given to the value of the cards.

## DEAL
The dealer shuffles the cards and deals four cards to each player, face down and one at a time.

## PLAY
Play in Pig is continuous, so instead of taking it in turns to play, the dealer shouts "Start!" or "Ready, set, go!" and the game begins. Players look at their cards to see if they have four of a kind.

**Players aim to collect four of a kind, such as these 10s.**

If not, they pass one card face down to the player on their left while at the same time receiving a card from the player to their right.

The game continues with players passing and receiving cards one by one. When a player collects four of a kind, that player stops passing and receiving cards, and touches their nose instead. All other players should immediately do the same. The last player to touch their nose is the pig and is out of the game.

The cards are collected up and a set removed. Then they are reshuffled and the game continues until there is only one person left in the game.

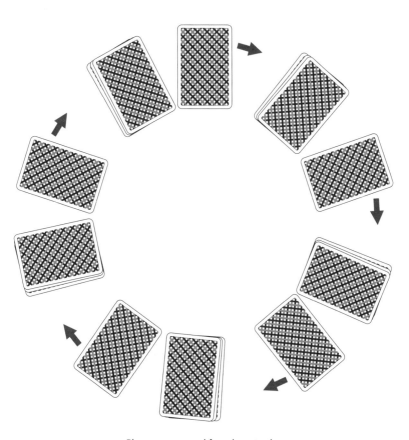

Players pass a card face down to the
player on their left while at the same
time receiving a face-down card from
the player on their right.

# SEQUENCE

Sequence is good for teaching young children the value of the cards in relation to each other and gives practice in putting cards in order according to rank. There's no skill required: you either have the card or you don't!

## WHAT YOU NEED
- Standard deck of cards
- Jokers removed

## CARDS
Aces are high.

## DEAL
Any player shuffles the cards and deals the whole deck, one at a time and face down. It doesn't matter if some players have more cards than others.

## PLAY
The player to the dealer's left puts down their lowest card face up on the table. Whoever has the next card going up in the sequence puts it down, and play continues until someone puts down an Ace in that suit. When the Ace is played, that player has to start another suit with their lowest card.

The winner is the first person to get rid of all their cards.

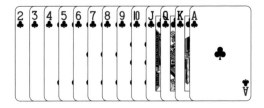

**Players put down their cards in sequence, starting with the lowest card up to the Ace.**

This fast-moving noisy game is best with three to four players. The goal is to win all the cards by slapping the Jack when it is turned up. Don't use your best cards for this as they're bound to get mussed up, and watch out—you might get your hand slapped in the process!

## WHAT YOU NEED
- Standard deck of cards
- Jokers removed

## DEAL

Any person deals out all the cards, one at a time, face down, to each player. It doesn't matter if some players have more cards than others. Players arrange their cards into a neat pile in front of them but do not look at them.

## PLAY

The player to the dealer's left lifts the top card of their pile and places it face up in the center of the table. The card must be turned over quickly and away from the player so that there is no unfair advantage where they see the card before the other players.

Moving clockwise, the player to the left of the first player lifts the top card of their pile and places it face up on

**Players turn their cards over quickly and away from them into the center of the table.**

Instructions continue on next page ➡

the card in the center of the table, turning it quickly and away from them as before. Play continues in this way with each player placing a card face up on the central pile until a Jack is turned up. At this point, the first player to slap the Jack wins the pile in the center of the table, and puts those cards face down underneath their own pile.

If a player runs out of cards, they try to slap the next Jack to stay in the game but if unsuccessful they are out.

If a player slaps a card by mistake, they have to give one of their cards as a penalty to the player whose card they slapped. If the player who slapped a card wrongly has run out of cards, they cannot try to slap the next Jack and are out of the game.

Play continues until one player has all the cards. The winner is the last person to slap a Jack, the others all having run out of cards.

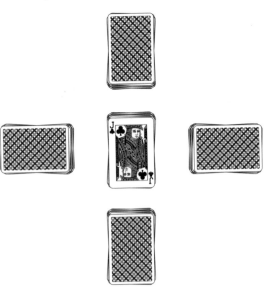

**When a Jack turns up, the first player to slap it wins the pile.**

In this speedy, boisterous game, the goal is to be first to spot matches and collect all the cards. Matching cards are those of the same rank—for example, two 7s or two Jacks (they don't have to match color).

## WHAT YOU NEED

- Standard deck of cards
- Jokers removed
- Two decks if more than three players

## DEAL

Any player deals out all the cards, face down and one at a time. It doesn't matter if some players have more cards than others. Players arrange their cards into a neat pile in front of them but do not look at them.

**Stock pile**          **Snap pile**

Each player has a stock and a snap pile in front of them.

## PLAY

Starting with the player on the left of the dealer and moving clockwise around the table, each player takes it in turn to take the top card from their stock and place it face up next to it to form a snap pile.

Play continues in this way. When a player sees that two cards on two snap piles match, they shout out "Snap!" They collect both snap piles and add them to the bottom of their stock pile.

Instructions continue
on next page ➡

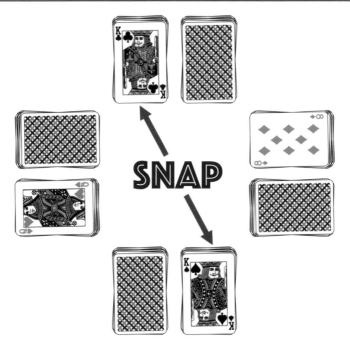

**The first person to shout "Snap!"
wins the snap piles.**

If a player shouts "Snap" when the cards don't match, they have to give every other player one card from their stock.

If two players shout "Snap!" at the same time, the two snap piles are combined and placed face up in the center of the table. Play continues as before. When a player turns up a card that matches the card in the center, the first person to shout "Snap" takes the cards.

If a player runs out of stock cards, they turn over their snap pile and continue. The winner is the one left with all the cards.

This fast, fun game is suitable for all ages. The goal is to be the first to get rid of all your cards, and it's all down to luck rather than skill.

### WHAT YOU NEED
- Standard deck of cards
- Jokers removed

### DEAL
Any player deals all the cards, face down and one at a time, to each player—it's fine if some players have more cards than others. Players pick up their cards and sort them so they match each other and are in order (e.g. two deuces, three 4s, one 7, and so on).

### PLAY
The player to the dealer's left places one card face up in the center of the table. If the next player to the left has a card of the same kind (rank), they place it on top and shout "Snip!" If they have another card that matches, they place it down too and shout "Snap!" If they

don't have a card that matches, play passes to the next player and the game continues.

The person who makes the third match shouts "Snorem!" and ends the round. That player now starts another round. The winner is the first person to get rid of all their cards.

A player's hand with cards sorted—this makes them easier to play.

Snip!

Snap!

Snorem!

# SPOONS

In this card-swapping game, similar to Pig (see page 22), when a player has four of a kind, everyone tries to grab a spoon. The player left without a spoon gets a penalty letter, and when they spell the word "spoon," they're out!

## WHAT YOU NEED
- Standard deck of cards
- Jokers removed
- Spoons, one fewer than the number of players (for example, if you have six players, you'll need five spoons)
- Pencil and paper

Put the spoons in the middle of the table.

## DEAL
Any player deals four cards to each player, face down and one at a time. The dealer puts the remaining cards in a face-down pile to form the stock.

## PLAY
Players look at their cards to see if they have four of a kind (very unlikely at this stage). The dealer takes the top card from the stock and adds it to their hand. The dealer discards one card and passes it face down to the player on their left. Play continues quickly around the table, with each player taking a card from the player on their right and deciding whether to keep it or pass it on.

The last player places their discarded card face down to form a discard pile. If the stock pile runs out during play, the dealer shuffles the discard pile and uses this as a new stock pile.

Play continues until a player gets four of a kind, at which point they can take a spoon from the middle of the table. All other players now race to pick up a spoon too. The player who failed to grab one gets a letter—the dealer writes the player's name on a piece of paper with the letter "S" underneath.

The dealer collects the cards, reshuffles, and deals again. The next round begins when the dealer takes another card from the stock pile.

Each time a player loses a round they get another letter, and they are out of the game when they spell out "spoon." Every time a player is eliminated, the dealer removes a spoon from the middle of the table. The winner is the last person left in the game.

Discard pile

Stock pile

Each player receives a card from
the player on their right.

Players discard a card to the
player on their left.

Players try to collect four of a kind
by swapping cards.

# STEALING BUNDLES

Also known as Steal the Pile, the object is to have the biggest "bundle" of cards at the end of the game by matching cards and stealing other players' bundles.

## WHAT YOU NEED
- Standard deck of cards
- Jokers removed

## DEAL
Any player deals four cards to each player, face down and one at a time. Four more cards are then dealt face up in the middle of the table. The rest of the cards are put face down to one side.

## PLAY
The player to the dealer's left looks at their cards to see if they have one that matches a card in the center—that is, of the same rank (the same number or picture). If they have, they take the card from the center and put it with their card in a face-up pile, or "bundle." If a player's card matches two or three center cards, they take all those cards and add them to their bundle.

Everyone takes a turn to play a card. If a player has a card that matches the top card of another player's bundle, they can steal that player's bundle and add it to their own!

If none of a player's cards match any center card, they must lay down one of their cards face up in the center.

When everyone has played their four cards, the dealer deals each player another four cards, face down, but none to the center. Play continues until all the cards have been played.

The winner is the player with the most cards in their bundle.

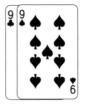 

**Players match cards to make bundles.**

PLAYER 1

PLAYER 2

    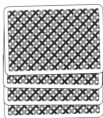

PLAYER 3

Initial layout for Stealing Bundles.

# WAR

A children's favorite for hundreds of years, this simple game requires only the ability to recognize the highest ranking out of two cards.
If three people want to play, remove one of the cards before dealing so that each player receives the same amount of cards.

## WHAT YOU NEED
- Standard deck of cards
- Jokers removed

## CARDS
Aces are high.

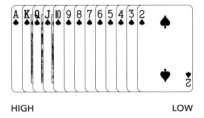

HIGH                                           LOW

Cards are ranked from high to low.

## DEAL
Any player deals out all the cards, one at a time and face down. Both players put their cards in a pile without looking at them.

## PLAY
Both players turn up the top cards of their respective piles and place them in the middle of the table. The highest card wins the hand, regardless of suit.

**PLAYER 1**

Player 2 wins the hand with the highest card (7 H).

**PLAYER 2**

The winner collects the cards and adds them face down to the bottom of their pile. If both cards in the middle are of equal value, the players go to war.

Both players take two more cards from the top of their stock piles and place one face down next to their first card in the middle of the table and the other face up on top of it. The highest card wins the hand and the winner collects all six cards. In the event of another tie, the war continues until a player turns up a winning card.

If a player runs out of cards in the middle of a war, their last card is turned face up and used as their card for the war. If there is another tie, the player who ran out of cards last time keeps that same card face up as the card they use while the other player continues to put down cards.

The aim is to win all the cards—if there's no winner within a set time limit, each player counts up the number of cards in their stock pile and the one with the most cards wins the game.

**PLAYER 1**

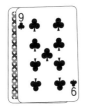 

**PLAYER 2**

Both players have turned up Aces so they go to war. Player 2 wins the hand by turning up 9 C and picks up all six cards.

**PLAYER 1**

**PLAYER 2**

Player 2 has run out of cards in the middle of the war, so 9 C is their last card. Player 1 continues to put down cards but cannot beat it so player 2 wins.

# GAMES FOR AGES 7+

The games in this chapter are suitable for mixed groups of adults and children from the age of seven or so. Players will learn more about matching and sequencing, and how to play cards onto building piles. They are also introduced to the concept of tricks and trump suits. Success doesn't just rely on the luck of the cards—a good memory and basic math skills will help, and there is a need for strategic thinking, too.

# CHEAT

Also known as I Doubt It, and Bluff, this game tests your ability to keep a straight face if bluffing about the cards you have—or to be able to spot when a player isn't being truthful! The aim is to be the first player to get rid of all their cards.

## WHAT YOU NEED
- Standard deck of cards
- Jokers removed
- Two decks if more than five players

## CARDS
Aces are low.

## DEAL
Any player shuffles the deck and deals out all the cards, one at a time and face down. All players should have the same number of cards—extra cards are placed face down in the center of the table to start a discard pile.

Players look at their cards and sort them into ranks.

## PLAY
The player to the dealer's left starts the game by placing all the Aces in their hand face down on the discard pile, saying what they have played—"One Ace," for example.

The next player then plays all the deuces that they have in their hand, the following player all the 3s, and so on, increasing rank all the time, with Aces following Kings.

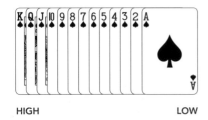

HIGH                                    LOW

Cards are ranked from high to low
—Ace is low.

Players organize their hands
according to rank (value) so the
cards are easier to play.

If a player doesn't have any suitable cards, they can say "Pass" and miss a turn, or they can attempt to cheat by laying down one to four cards and declaring them to be the cards that are required. A player can also lie about the number of cards they are putting down, if they think that they can get away with it.

If anyone doubts another player's declaration, they shout "Cheat!" and that player must turn over the cards they just put down. If the player was

cheating, they have to pick up the whole discard pile. If the cards match what the player said, the challenger has to pick up the discard pile.

The player who picks up all the cards restarts the game. The game ends when a player gets rid of all their cards.

In a multiplayer game, it is less likely that a player would have four of a kind, so another player might issue a challenge. In this case, they'd be wrong and would have to pick up the whole discard pile.

A player can lie about the number of cards they're putting down—saying, "Two 6s" here, for example.

# CRAZY EIGHTS

Also known as Rockaway, or Swedish Rummy, 8s are wild (or crazy) in this game, meaning they can represent any card or suit. The goal is to be the first to get rid of all your cards.

## WHAT YOU NEED
- Standard deck of cards
- Jokers removed
- Two decks if more than five players
- Pencil and paper to keep score (optional)

## CARDS
Aces are low. Eights are wild cards and can represent any number or suit. If scoring, 8s and face cards are penalty cards if left in a player's hand.

## DEAL
Any player deals seven cards to each player, one at a time and face down. Deal five cards if there are more than two players. The remainder of the cards are placed face down in the middle of the table as the stock pile. The dealer turns the top card of the stock pile over to start a discard pile next to it.

## PLAY
The player to the dealer's left has to match the face-up card by putting down a card of the same number or suit. This goes on top of the discard pile and the next player has to match this card.

Eights are wild and can be used for any number or suit. For example, if you can't match the card on top of the discard pile but you do have an 8 of clubs, you can put this down and change the suit to hearts if you have a lot of those. The next player must then match the card to the suit or rank the 8 was meant to cover.

If you can't match the card, take a card from the stock pile until you find one that you can put down. You can also draw from the stock when it's your turn even if you can put down a card—it's worth holding onto a crazy 8 until you are close to going out of the game.

If the stock runs out before the game has finished, shuffle the discard pile and use this to continue play. The winner is the first person to get rid of all their cards.

Eights can represent any number or suit.

The cards in the discard pile have been spread out here to show you who played which card. Player 1 put down 4 C, player 2 followed suit with 5 C. Player 3 matched rank with 5 D. Player 4 couldn't match this card so played a crazy 8 and changed the suit to spades. Player 5 has followed suit.

Eights and face cards incur penalty points
if left in a player's hand.

### SCORING (OPTIONAL)

Cards left in the hands of non-winning players are scored as follows: 8s = 50, face cards = 10, and all other cards are face value. These points are awarded to the winner of the round. The first person to reach a specific number of points wins the game (for two players, 100 points, three players, 150 points, and thereafter increasing by 50 points for each player).

# EGYPTIAN RAT SCREW

Combining elements of Beggar My Neighbor (see page 12) and Slapjack (see page 25), this game relies on luck and fast reactions. The aim is to get hold of all the cards.

## WHAT YOU NEED
- Standard deck of cards
- Jokers removed
- Two decks if more than six players

## CARDS
Aces and face cards are challenge cards—the next player puts down up to four cards for an Ace, three for a King, two for a Queen, and one for a Jack. Players can slap the pile and claim it if one of various card combinations is played (see opposite page).

## DEAL
Any player deals all the cards, face down and one at a time, to each player. It doesn't matter if some players have more cards than others. Players arrange their cards into a neat pile.

## PLAY
The person on the dealer's left places their top card face up in the middle of the table. The next player places their top card on top of this. Play continues clockwise around the table, each player placing one card on top of the other, until an Ace or a face card is played.

This is now a challenge: the next player has a number of chances to play another Ace or face card. If they fail to turn up one of these cards, the challenger takes the face-up pile and adds it to the bottom of their stock pile. If the player turns up another Ace or face card, the next player after them must beat it.

## SLAPPING
Players agree beforehand on various card combinations where the fastest player can slap the pile during play and claim it. The most common are:

**Double**: two of a kind

**Sandwich**: two of a kind with a card of different value in between

**Tens**: two cards played consecutively add up to ten

**Four of a kind**: four cards of the same rank

**Marriage**: King and Queen.

If you slap incorrectly, you must add two cards to the bottom of the face-up pile. You can stay in the game and continue to slap even if you've run out of cards.

Any Ace or face card is a challenge card.

Double

Marriage

Tens

Sandwich

Four of a kind

If one of these combinations turn up,
the fastest player to slap the pile wins it.

The winner is the player who ends up
with all the cards.

# GAPS

Also known as Vacancies and Stops, this solitaire game relies on skill rather than just luck. The object is to arrange the cards in suits, in sequence from deuce to King, with deuce on the far left and King at the far right.

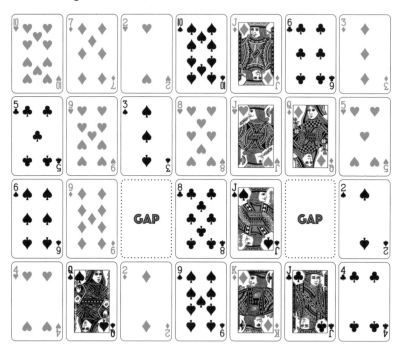

## WHAT YOU NEED

- Standard deck of cards
- Jokers removed

## DEAL

Shuffle the cards then deal them all in four rows, face up. Remove the Aces.

## PLAY

Fill any space with a card next higher in rank and in the same suit as the card on the left. Fill an empty space at the left end of a row with a deuce. A space to the right of a King can't be filled, but if that King can be moved to come after

Deal all the cards face up in four rows and remove the Aces to make gaps.
If 4 D moves to the right of 3 D, 10 C moves to the right of 9 C and
4 H moves to the right of 3 H, freeing up a space to start
the bottom row with any deuce.

its proper Queen, that gap may open up
again. Play continues until the position
of the four Kings blocks the game.

You are allowed two more deals.
Gather up all the cards in the layout
that aren't in their correct sequence

behind deuces and shuffle these along
with the Aces. Deal the cards out again
to fill the rows, remove the Aces as
before, and continue.

# GO BOOM

Go Boom is a good introduction to trick-taking games (a trick is a group of cards, one from each player in turn). The highest card in the suit that was first put down wins the trick.

### WHAT YOU NEED
- Standard deck of cards
- Jokers removed
- Pencil and paper to keep score (optional)

### CARDS
Aces are high, deuces are low. Ace and face cards are penalty cards if scoring.

### DEAL
Any player shuffles the deck and deals seven cards to each player, one at a time and face down. The rest of the cards are placed face down in a pile in the center of the table to form the stock.

### PLAY
Players look at their cards and the player to the dealer's left puts down the first card. Players must play a card in the same suit or of the same value (rank). If a player is unable to do this, they draw a card from the stock, one at a time, until they get a card that can be played. Players take it in turns to play a card and play is clockwise.

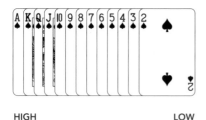

HIGH                                    LOW

Cards ranked from high to low.

In this trick player 2 doesn't have any spades but has put down Q C because it is the same rank as Q S. The Ace of spades is the highest card and wins the trick.

If a player uses up all the stock pile without finding a card they can play, they have to pass.

The player who put down the highest card in the suit that was first put down wins the trick and gets to start the next one.

Play continues until a player gets rid of all their cards and says "Boom!"

## WINNING THE GAME

Players can decide either to play a number of rounds or to score penalty points for cards left in hand, which are credited to the winner. Players left with cards in their hand are penalized as follows: Ace = 1 point, face cards = 10 points, all other cards their face value. These points are awarded to the winner. The first player to reach 100 points, say, wins the game.

Although there are two high cards of the same rank here, K H wins because it's in the suit that was led.

If scoring, players left with penalty cards in their hand are penalized—Ace = 1 point, face cards = 10 points, all other cards their face value, which are given to the person who won the round.

# GOLF

Just like in the game golf, players try to get the lowest score possible by swapping cards. Players have to guess whether a hidden card is of higher or lower value than the card they have picked up.

## WHAT YOU NEED
- Standard deck of cards
- Jokers removed
- Two decks if more than four players
- Pencil and paper to keep score

## DEAL
Each player is dealt six cards, one at a time and face down. The remaining cards are placed face down in a pile in the middle of the table to form the stock pile. The top card of the stock is turned over and placed beside it to form a discard pile.

Players arrange their cards in two rows in front of them and turn over any two cards.

## PLAY
The player to the dealer's left begins, and the turn to play passes clockwise. A player either picks up the top card from the stock pile or the top card

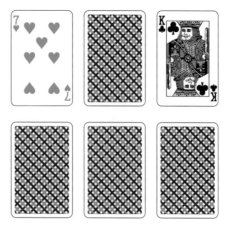

A player's initial layout before play commences.

from the discard pile. A card picked up from the discard pile must be used immediately. The player may use the card drawn to replace any of the cards in their layout, but if the player is replacing a face-down card they may not look at it first.

The round ends as soon as a player has all their cards face up. All other players turn over any hidden cards and the hands are then scored.

## SCORING

Ace is 1 point, deuce is minus 2 points, 3 to 10 are face value, Jack and Queen are 10 points, Kings are 0. Two cards of the same rank in a row score 0 points for the row, even if the cards of the same rank are deuces. The player who has the lowest score after nine rounds, or "holes," wins.

This hand scores 8 points—the King counts for 0 and the two 5s mean the bottom row scores 0 points.

# GOPS

The rules for GOPS (Game of Pure Strategy) are easy enough to learn, but to become proficient a player needs a good memory of cards played and an ability to bluff. Players make bids to win the greatest value of diamonds.

### WHAT YOU NEED
- Standard deck of cards
- Jokers and all the hearts removed

### CARDS
Aces are high when bidding. Ace of diamonds is low for scoring.

### DEAL
One player takes all the spades and the other all the clubs. Either player shuffles the diamonds well and places the diamond pile face down in the middle. The top card is turned up.

**PLAYER 1**

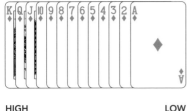

HIGH                                    LOW

Diamonds are the valuable suit but Ace is low.

Diamonds

**PLAYER 2**

Players bid for the diamonds by selecting a card and placing it face down in front of them.

## PLAY

Each player looks at their hand and secretly bids for the diamond card by placing a card face down in front of them.

When both players are ready, the face-down cards are turned over and the player who put down the highest ranking card wins the diamond and puts it to one side. The two black cards are discarded and play continues in the same way for the next 12 diamond cards. If both players put down the same card, this is a tie and the diamond is left untaken. The next diamond card is then turned up and the winner of the next bid wins both diamond cards.

## SCORE

King of diamonds is worth 13 points, Queen 12, Jack 11. Ace to 10 are face value, with 91 points in all to be won. The player with the most points wins.

PLAYER 1

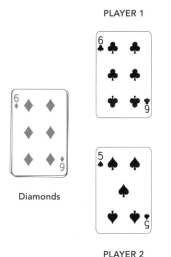

Diamonds

PLAYER 2

Player 1 wins the diamonds.

The highest value diamonds are the face cards.

# HEARTS

In this fun trick-taking game, players try to avoid winning hearts, usually by losing tricks. The goal is to score the fewest points, and the game is best with four players.

## WHAT YOU NEED
- Standard deck of cards
- Jokers removed
- Pencil and paper to keep score

## CARDS

Aces are high. Hearts are penalty cards. So that cards can be distributed evenly, if there are three players, remove the deuce of diamonds. If five players, remove the deuce of diamonds and deuce of clubs; if six players, remove all the deuces; if seven players, remove the deuce of diamonds, clubs, and spades.

## DEAL

Cut the cards to see who deals first. The deal passes to the left after each round. The dealer shuffles the deck and deals out all the cards, one at a time and face down.

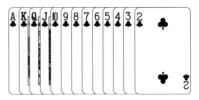

**HIGH**　　　　　　　　　　　　**LOW**

Ranking of cards from high to low—
Ace is highest.

Remove enough deuces to make
the deal come out even.

Player 3 doesn't have any spades
so gets rid of a high hearts card
(player 1 takes the trick).

## PLAY

The player with the deuce of clubs (3 C if five, six, or seven players) starts the game by laying down the first card, which can be any card. Other players must follow suit. If a player does not have a card in that suit they may discard any other card, and this is a good opportunity to get rid of a hearts card.

The highest card of the suit that was first laid down wins the trick, and the player places it face down in front of them. The winner leads the next trick. A player cannot lead with a heart until a heart has been discarded in a previous trick.

A player leads with a low heart to force another player to pick up some penalty cards.

Each hearts card scores one penalty point.

## SCORING

Each hearts card captured incurs a penalty point—there are 13 penalty points overall (unless the deuce has been removed for a six-player game). The winner is the player who has the lowest score when a target point is reached, or after a certain number of rounds.

# JAMES BOND

In this speedy swapping game, players race to be the first to get four of a kind in all their piles. Because everyone plays at once, the first player to touch a card in the middle gets to pick it up, so you'll need to be quick off the mark.

## WHAT YOU NEED
- Standard deck of cards
- Jokers removed

## DEAL
Any player shuffles the cards and deals four cards face up into the center of the table. The dealer then deals the cards face down into piles of four and gives six piles to two players, four to three players, and three piles to four players.

## PLAY
The dealer says "Ready, set, go!" and players all start playing at once. A player picks up one of their piles and may swap a card with one in the middle to get four of a kind. For example, if a player has three cards that are all a 7 and there is a 7 in the middle, they can discard the card from their pile that isn't a 7 and pick up the 7 from the middle.

A player can only have four cards in their hand at one time, so must always discard to the center before picking up another card.

A player can put down a pile and pick up another one at any time, but may only look at one pile at a time.

If a player doesn't need any of the cards that are in the center of the table, they may have to wait for another player to put down a card they can use.

The first person to have four of a kind in all their piles shouts "James Bond!" and turns their piles face up to win.

Examples of four of a kind.

A player would swap Q H for 10 C in the
middle to make four of a kind.

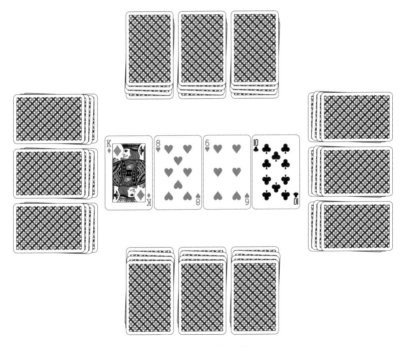

Layout if there are four players.

# KARMA

Also known as Palace, the goal is to get rid of your cards on the discard pile and be the first to run out of cards.

## WHAT YOU NEED

- Standard deck of cards
- Jokers removed
- Two decks if three or more players

## CARDS

Aces are high, 3s are lowest. Deuces and 10s are wild cards—a deuce resets the cards to this number, and a 10 takes the discard pile out of the game. A player who puts down a 10 can follow this with any card they like. Four of the same rank takes the discard pile out of the game too, and the player who completed the set of four gets to play again.

## DEAL

The dealer deals three cards at a time to each player, face down and in a row. The dealer then deals each person six more cards face down. Players look at these cards and place three face up on the face-down cards in front of them. The other three cards are the hand.

The remainder of the cards go face down into the center of the table to form the stock pile.

## PLAY

The dealer turns over the top card of the stock and places it face up next to it to form the discard pile.

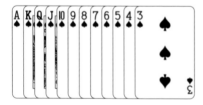

HIGH                                              LOW

Cards ranked from high to low.

Any deuce resets the cards to this number.

Any 10 takes the discard pile out of the game.

## PLAYING

The player to the left of the dealer plays a card that is equal to or higher than the start card (multiple cards can be put down as long as they are of the same rank). A player must always have at least three cards in their hand so draws cards from the stock to replace the one(s) put down. If a player can't put down a card, they pick up the whole discard pile.

## FACE-UP CARDS

Players move to their face-up cards when they have played everything from their hand. If they can't play a card, they have to pick up the discard pile and use that up before they can play again from their cards on the table.

## FACE-DOWN CARDS

When a player has got rid of all their face-up cards, they flip over one of their face-down cards onto the discard pile. If it is equal or higher than the top discard it can be played; otherwise the player must pick up the discard pile and get rid of it before playing their face-down cards.

The winner is the first person to get rid of their face-up and face-down cards.

Four of a kind—either as a combination of plays or all at the same time—takes the discard pile out of the game.

Each player is dealt nine cards. Six are laid out in rows as shown and three are in the hand.

# KLONDIKE

Also known as Patience, the goal is to build all four suits on the Aces in sequence. The important thing is to uncover the face-down cards and bring them into play as soon as you can.

## WHAT YOU NEED
- Standard deck of cards
- Jokers removed

## CARDS
Aces are low.

## DEAL
The player shuffles the cards thoroughly then deals 28 cards in seven piles in a layout known as the tableau. Lay the cards out as follows: the first pile has one card, the second two, the third three, and so on. The last card of each pile is face up and all the others are face down. These are the building piles.

## PLAY
Start by moving the face-up cards in the tableau to build them on each other—cards must be one rank lower and the opposite color of the card it is being placed on. Spread the cards downward (see opposite page) so you can read them. When two or more cards are built on another pile, you move them as a unit.

As you move cards from one building pile to another, turn over the next face-down card in that pile. If there is an empty space in the tableau, only a king may fill this.

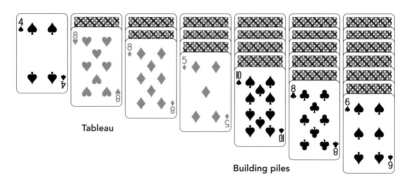

Tableau

Building piles

Set out seven building piles in your layout (tableau).

**Base cards**                                    **Stock**     **Discard pile**

The Aces form the base cards.

Turn over the stock,
three cards at a time,
to continue playing.

The four Aces form the base
cards or foundations. When they
are turned up they are placed in
a row above the building cards
and other cards can be played
on them if in the same suit,
going up in sequence.

**Base cards**

When you have done all the
building you can on the Aces
and the building piles, you may
use the stock. Turn the stock
over three cards at a time and
put the turned up cards to form
a discard or waste pile. You
may also play off the top of the
discard pile. If the stock runs out,
turn over the discard pile to form
a new stock and keep going.

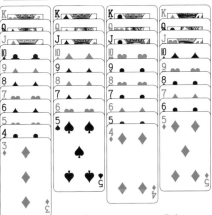

You win the game if you get all
the cards out and can play in
sequence onto the base cards.

The game is won—all the
cards are out.

# LINGER LONGER

This is a good game for learning about tricks and trump suits (special suits that outrank any other). A card from a trump suit always beats those of other suits. Here players aim to be the last person left in the game—the one to linger longer!

## WHAT YOU NEED
- Standard deck of cards
- Jokers removed

## CARDS

Aces are high. Dealer's last card dealt determines trump suit.

A K Q J 10 9 8 7 6 5 4 3 2 ♥

Cards ranked from high to low.

## DEAL

Any player deals the same number of cards as there are players—for example, six players will get six cards each. Cards are dealt one at a time and face down. The dealer shows their last card to the other players—this card's suit will be the trump suit—and then adds this card to their hand. The rest of the cards are put face down in a pile on the table to form the stock pile.

The dealer's last card sets the trump suit (here, diamonds) and is shown to the other players.

## PLAY

The player to the dealer's left puts down a card (this is called "leading to the first trick"). Play passes clockwise, with players laying down one card each to complete the trick, following suit if possible. If a player cannot follow suit they can play a trump card or any other card.

The trick is won by the person who put down the highest card of the leading suit, or the highest trump card. The winner puts the trick to one side, takes a card from the stock pile, and starts the next trick.

Play continues as long as players have cards in their hand. If you're out of cards, you're out of the game.

Player 1 leads with J S. Player 5 wins the trick with the highest card to follow suit by playing A S.

Player 1 leads the trick with J H. Despite player 4 putting down the Ace, player 5 has no hearts to play so wins the trick with a low trump (3 D).

# NERTS

Also known as Pounce or Racing Demon, this rapid game can be played by up to eight people (if you have the space). The aim is to get rid of your Nerts pile and play as many cards as you can into the center of the table.

## WHAT YOU NEED
- One deck of cards per player—ones with different backs
- Jokers removed
- Pencil and paper to keep score

## CARDS
Aces are low.

## DEAL
Each player shuffles their deck and deals themselves 12 cards face down and one face up in a single pile—this is the Nerts pile (or Demon). Four more cards (building piles) are dealt face up in a row next to this pile. The remaining cards form a stock.

## PLAY
When all players are ready, one person shouts "Go!" and play begins.

Everyone plays at the same time, putting cards into the center of the table or onto their own building piles as fast as they can.

Players move cards from their Nerts pile or turn cards over from their stock, three at a time, until they find one that they can play. Cards turned over from the stock form a discard pile.

If you run out of stock cards, turn the discard pile over to form a new stock.

Nerts pile                    Building piles

Each player lays out a 13-card Nerts pile and four face-up building piles in front of them.

Stock pile

If a player has an Ace, they put it face up in the center of the table, where it becomes a base card, or foundation. Anyone can build on this card if they have the next card in the suit.

**Aces are base cards and go face up in the center of the table. Any player can build on them by placing the next card higher in the sequence, in the same suit.**

To play onto the four building piles, the cards must be one rank lower and the opposite color of the card it is being placed on. Players can also move cards from one building card pile to another—to fill any gaps this causes, replace with the top card from the Nerts pile.

A player shouts "Nerts!" (or "Out!") when they have used up all the cards in the Nerts pile, and everyone stops playing.

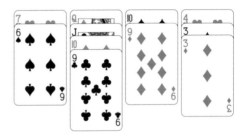

**Cards must be in descending order and alternating colors when placed on the building piles.**

## SCORING

Players score as follows:

- 10 points to the person who called "Nerts!"
- All other players lose 1 point for each card left in their Nerts piles.

- Each player gets 1 point for every card they played on the foundation cards.

Further hands are played until a player reaches a target score (usually 100).

# NIFTY 50

An easy game to learn and play, the goal is to collect the most cards. It's a great game for practicing basic equations by adding, subtracting, multiplying, or dividing the numbers on three cards to reach 50. If your child struggles with mathematics, encourage them to write the problems on a piece of paper. As their skills and confidence improve, they may no longer need to do this.

## WHAT YOU NEED
- Standard deck of cards
- Jokers removed
- Pencil and paper to keep score

Aces counts for 1, Kings are 13, Queens 12, and Jacks 11. All other cards equal their face value.

## CARDS
Aces are low and count for 1. Numbered cards equal their face value. Jacks are 11, Queens are 12, and Kings are 13—or make each face card count for 10 if you want to make it easier. If there are three players, remove four cards and set these aside before dealing the rest of the cards.

**PLAYER 1**

## DEAL
Any player deals all the cards, one at a time and face down, until each player has the same amount of cards.

**PLAYER 2**

## PLAY
Each player arranges their cards into a neat face-down stock pile in front of them. Play is

Player 1 can tally their cards as 9 x 7 – 12 = 51; player 2's tally is 13 (King) + 11 (Jack) = 24 x 2 = 48.

consecutive rather than taking turns. Each player turns over three cards from the top of their piles and adds, divides, subtracts, or multiplies the numbers to reach 50. They can move the cards around if it helps to do the math.

The player whose total is closest to 50 wins all the cards and puts them in a discard pile next to them. If there is a tie, both players keep their cards and add them to their discard pile.

**VARIANT**

Players can combine cards to form a two-digit number—e.g., 3 + 2 = 32—which will enable them to make more equations and is helpful if they have low cards. Players need to agree that this is allowed before the game begins. Each player then draws three more cards from their stock and does another equation. When all the cards from the stock piles have been played, the game ends. The winner is the player with the most cards in their discard pile.

PLAYER 1

Discard pile

PLAYER 2

If combining cards to form a two-digit number, player 1's hand can be tallied at 11 + 42 = 53, player 2's as 63 – 10 = 53 (a tie).

# NINETY-NINE

This is great for practicing mental mathematics! Cards are laid down in a running total, and the goal is to avoid going over 99. Certain cards have special properties, which may vary depending on the version of the game you're playing.

## WHAT YOU NEED
- Standard deck of cards
- Jokers removed
- Three tokens per player (such as buttons, coins, toothpicks)

## CARDS
- Most number cards have face value
- Aces can be 1 or 11
- 4s have no value but reverse the direction of play
- 9s have no value
- 10s subtract 10
- Jacks and Queens are worth 10
- A King takes the total to 99, or keeps it there if the total is already 99

## DEAL

Any player deals three cards to each player, face down and one at a time. The rest of the cards are placed face down in the middle of the table to form the stock. Each player takes three tokens.

## PLAY

The player to the dealer's left places one card face up next to the stock and announces the value of their card. They then take another card from the stock so that they still have three cards in their hand.

Players take it in turns and play passes clockwise. After each card is played, the player announces the new total and then draws another card from the stock.

If a player cannot put down a card without taking the total over 99, that player loses the round and forfeits one token.

At the end of each round the deal passes to the left and the cards are reshuffled by the next dealer. When a player loses all three tokens they are out of the game. The winner is the last player left with a token.

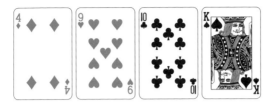

Several cards have special functions in this game—4s
count for zero but reverse the direction of play; 9s count
for zero; 10s take off 10, and a King takes the total to 99.

Each player starts off with three
tokens and maintains three cards
in their hands during play.

The running total so far is 24: 9 has no
value and 10 takes away 10.

The King instantly takes the running
total to 99. The next player has to
put down another King, a 10, a 9,
or a 4 to stay in the round.

# PLAY OR PAY

In this game, players put down cards in sequence in each of the four suits. Each deal is one round, and players decide beforehand how many rounds to play. The winner is the one with the most counters.

## WHAT YOU NEED
- Standard deck of cards
- Jokers removed
- 20 counters per player (such as buttons, coins, toothpicks)

## CARDS
Ace can be high or low, and sequences can go "round-the-corner," whereby the King and deuce both connect with the Ace—for example, JQKA23.

## ANTE
Each player puts one counter in the middle of the table (the "pot") before each deal.

## DEAL
Any player deals all the cards, one at a time and face down. If a player has fewer cards than other players they should put another counter in the pot.

Both King and deuce can connect with the Ace.

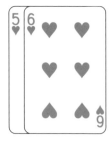

Player 1 starts with 5 H—the next card put down is 6 H as it is the next in the sequence in the same suit.

## PLAY

Players take turns and play moves clockwise around the table. The player to the dealer's left puts down any card. The next player must put down the next card in sequence in the same suit—if unable to do so, they put another counter in the pot.

Whoever plays the 13th card in a suit may start another suit.

All cards played remain face up on the table.

Play continues until a player gets rid of all their cards. The other players put a counter in the pot for each card left in their hand, and the winner takes the pot. If a player uses all their counters, they're out of the game. The winner is the one with the most counters after an agreed number of rounds.

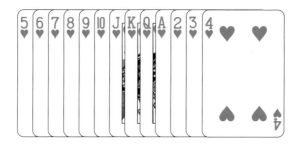

When all 13 cards are on the table, another suit may be started.

# ROLLING STONE

This simple trick-taking game can be a lot of fun but also very frustrating—just when you think you're about to get rid of all your cards you have to pick up a whole heap more!

## WHAT YOU NEED
- Standard deck of cards
- Jokers removed

## CARDS
Aces are high.
There should be eight cards for each player: if four players, use AKQJT987 of each suit. If five play, add the 6s and 5s; if six, add the 4s and 3s.

## DEAL
Any player deals the cards, one at a time and face down, so that each player has eight cards.

## PLAY
Players look at their cards and sort them into suits so that they are easier to play. The player to the dealer's left may lead the first trick (put down the first card) with any card, which is placed in the middle of the table. The turn to play passes clockwise, with players following suit if possible. If everyone follows suit, the cards are put in a discard pile and the player of the highest card starts the next round.

If a player cannot follow suit, they must pick up all the cards played so far and add them to their hand. That player then leads the next round, but has to put down a card in a different suit.

The winner is the first player to get rid of all their cards.

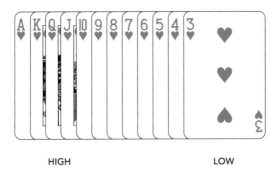

HIGH                                    LOW

When deciding who has won the trick,
the cards rank as shown.

Each player has eight cards—they sort
their hands into suits so the cards are
easier to play.

Player 3 couldn't follow suit so has
to pick up all the cards.

# RUMMY

This easy-to-learn game is hugely popular the world over, and there are many variants. The goal is to be the first out of the game by matching (melding) all their cards, thereby winning points from other players. Set a target before you start playing—for example, the winner is the first to reach 300 points, or the player with the most points by a set time.

## WHAT YOU NEED
- Standard deck of cards
- Jokers removed
- Pencil and paper to keep score

## CARDS
Aces are low and worth 1 point; Jacks, Queens, and Kings are all worth 10 points. All other cards are face value.

Also known as "matched sets," melds are made by sequencing three or more cards of the same suit, or by grouping three or more cards of the same kind.

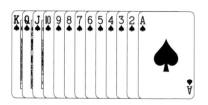

Cards ranked from high to low. K, Q, and J score 10 each; Ace scores 1.

You need at least three cards in a melded sequence, which must be next to each other in rank and in the same suit. Ace can only be used in a low meld (A, 2, 3) not with a Q and K.

Three (or four) of a kind makes a meld.

## DEAL

Choose the first dealer. The dealer deals the cards face down and one at a time as follows: ten cards to two players; seven cards to three to four players; six cards to five to six players. The remaining cards form the stock pile, which is placed on the table. The dealer turns over the top card and places it face up next to the stock pile to start the discard pile.

## PLAY

Players look at their hands and sort their cards. The player to the dealer's left either draws the top card from the stock or picks up the upcard (from the top of the discard pile).

A player can place any melds down on the table before discarding a card to end their turn. If they picked up the upcard at the start of their turn, they must discard a different card.

Play moves clockwise around the table. Players lay down melds and add cards to melds put down by other players or add to their own melds (this is called "laying off"). Players cannot lay off cards if they haven't yet put down any melds.

The discard pile is turned over if the stock runs out and used as a new stock pile—it must not be shuffled.

Play ends when a player goes out by using up all their cards, with or without a final discard. The turn to deal now passes to the left.

Stock pile       Discard pile

The top card of the stock pile is flipped over to start a discard pile.

A player sorts their hand into melds.

Instructions continue on next page
➡

# RUMMY CONTINUED

## GOING RUMMY

A player "goes rummy" if they put down all the cards in their hand at the same time, without any previous melding or laying off of melds.

## SCORING

When a player goes out, their score is the combined value of the cards left in their opponents' hands. Points are doubled if the player has gone rummy.

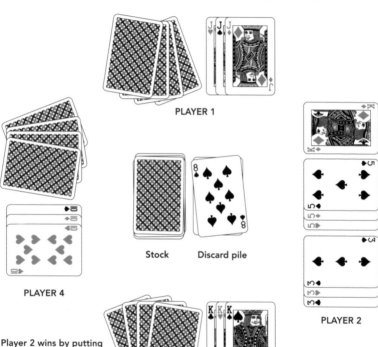

PLAYER 1

Stock

Discard pile

PLAYER 4

PLAYER 2

PLAYER 3

Player 2 wins by putting down two melds, laying off against player 3's meld of Kings (shown next to player 2 for ease of reference, but in a live game this would be added to the meld), and discarding 8 S.

**PLAYER 1**

**PLAYER 3**

**PLAYER 4**

All the points on the cards left in the
other players' hands are added up and
given to player 2—here, 89 points.

# RUMMY 500

Also known as 500 Rum and Pinochle Rummy (among other names), this is the same as basic Rummy (see page 72), except that players score points for melds put down as well as for going out. Players can also pick up all or some of the discard pile rather than just the top card.

## WHAT YOU NEED

- Standard deck of cards
- Jokers removed
- Two decks if more than four players
- Pencil and paper to keep score

## CARDS

Aces rank high or low, not both at once. They count for 1 if melded in a low sequence (Ace, deuce, 3) but otherwise is worth 15 points; Jacks, Queens, and Kings are worth 10 points. All other cards are face value.

Also known as "matched sets," melds are at least three of a kind, or at least three of a sequence in the same suit.

## DEAL

Choose the first dealer. The deal passes to the left after each round. The dealer deals seven cards, one at a time and face down, to each player. The remaining cards form the stock pile. The dealer turns over the top card and places it face up next to the stock to form the discard pile.

Players look at their hands and sort their cards to start making melds.

## PLAY

The player to the left of the dealer starts with taking a card from the stock or discard pile. A player can take the whole, or part, of the discard pile, so long as they immediately put down the last card they picked up as part of a meld.

A player can place any melds down on the table before discarding a card to end their turn.

The discard pile should be slightly spread out as cards are laid down so that players can see what cards are in it.

Play moves clockwise around the table, with players laying down melds and adding cards to existing melds ("laying off"). When a player adds to another player's meld, they keep that card by their side so it's easier to add up the score at the end of the round.

If the stock runs out before the end of the round, turn over the discard pile and use this as a new stock pile—but do not shuffle it. Play ends when a player goes out by using up all their cards, with or without a final discard.

If the stock runs out, play continues with players drawing from the discard pile until a player fails to pick up from this pile.

Aces can rank high or low.

Unless melded in a low sequence, an Ace is worth 15 points—including if it's left in a player's hand at the end of the round!

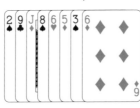

Players can see what cards are in the discard pile and judge whether to pick up some, all, or nothing from it when it's their turn.

Instructions continue on next page ➡

# RUMMY 500 CONTINUED

## SCORING

Each player counts up the points of the cards they have melded less the value of the cards left in their hand, resulting in a plus or minus score. The first player to score 500 is the winner of the game.

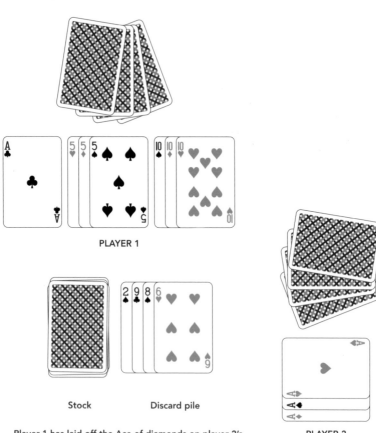

PLAYER 1

Stock          Discard pile

Player 1 has laid off the Ace of diamonds on player 2's meld of Aces (other players are not shown).

PLAYER 2

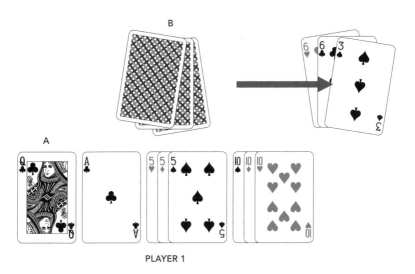

PLAYER 1

Another player has gone out so all players count up their scores. Player 1 adds up the value of their melded cards (A = 70) minus the value of the cards left in their hand (B = 15). Player 1's score is 55.

# SEVENS

Also known as Fan Tan, Card Dominoes, or Parliament, the goal is to be the first to get rid of all your cards. Strategy can be key here—hold onto the 6s, 7s, and 8s for as long as possible to block other players. But if these numbers are your only playable cards, you must put them down!

### WHAT YOU NEED
- Standard deck of cards
- Jokers removed
- Pencil and paper to keep score

### CARDS
Aces are low and can only be played after a deuce.

### DEAL
Any player deals all the cards, one at a time and face down. The cards may be dealt unequally but this doesn't matter so long as the deal moves to the left after each round and everyone deals a hand.

### PLAY
Players look at their cards and sort them into suits and rank to make them easier to play.

The player with the 7 of diamonds starts the round by laying it face up on the table. The next player adds a card in the same suit and in sequential order—either under the 7 (going up) or on top of the 7 (going down).

The only way a new suit layout can be started is with a 7, which a player can put down at any turn. Each player takes

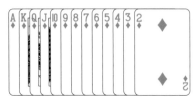

Cards ranked from high to low.

Players sort their hands into suits and rank.

**Play starts with 7 D.**

**Next card in sequence going down.**

**Next card in sequence going up.**

it in turn to put down one card and can add to the top or bottom of any stack.

If a player can't play a card they pass and the turn goes to the next player.

Play stops with the first person to get rid of all their cards. Each player gets a point for every card left in their hand. Once everyone has had a chance to deal, add the points up and the overall winner is the player with the smallest score.

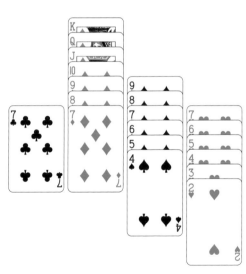

**Example of round in progress.**

# SPIT

The goal in Spit (also known as Speed) is to get rid of all your layout cards as quickly as possible by placing them on the spit piles. You can only use one hand and play is continuous rather than by turn, so you'll need to be lightning-quick!

## WHAT YOU NEED
- Standard deck of cards
- Jokers removed

## DEAL

Any dealer deals all the cards, one at a time and face down, to each player.

Each player deals five stock piles of cards in a row, face down, into a solitaire-style layout known as the tableau. The first pile has one card, the second two, and so on, until the last pile has five cards. Turn over the last card in each stock pile. The remaining 11 cards are the spit cards and are kept face down in a pile. Players must not look at their spit cards before they are played.

## PLAY

When both players are ready they turn over the top cards on the spit cards, placing them in the middle of the table between the two tableaus. The aim is to play the 15 cards from the stock piles in the tableaus onto the spit piles. Players play continuously rather than taking turns.

A card moved to a spit pile must be the next in sequence—either up or down. It doesn't matter if it's in the same suit or not, and it can be played on either spit pile. When a player moves a face-up card onto a spit pile, they may turn over the next card in the stock pile.

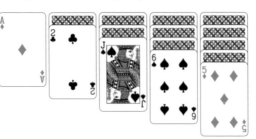

The tableau, with five stock piles.

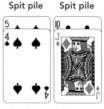

Cards moved onto a spit pile must be next in sequence but can be up or down, and in any suit.

If a face-up pile is emptied, because they have played a card into the spit pile, the player may move a card from another pile into the space. When neither player can play any more cards, they both shout "Spit!" and turn over the next spit cards face up onto the spit piles. Play then resumes.

The first person to empty their stock piles wins the round. If both players run out of spit cards but haven't managed to empty their stock piles, the player

with the fewest cards left wins the round. The winner of the round takes the smallest spit pile, the loser the other. Both add these to their unplayed cards, shuffle them, and lay them out in the tableau to start another round.

Whenever one player has fewer than 15 cards at the start of a new round they lay out the cards as far as possible, but there will now only be one communal spit pile. The winner is the first person to get rid of all their cards.

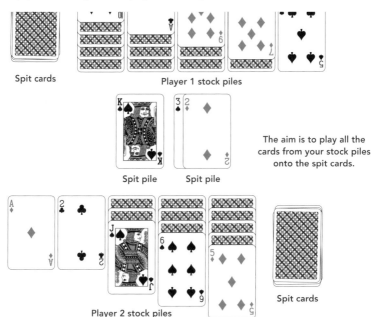

Spit cards

Player 1 stock piles

Spit pile    Spit pile

The aim is to play all the cards from your stock piles onto the spit cards.

Player 2 stock piles

Spit cards

# SWITCH

Also known as Two Four Jacks, Irish Switch, and Last Card, this game has several "trick" or "power" cards that affect play, making it similar to Uno. The aim is to be the first player to get rid of all their cards.

## WHAT YOU NEED

- Standard deck of cards
- Jokers removed
- Two decks if more than five players

## CARDS

**Ace**: This switches to a different suit, which the player nominates.

**Deuce**: The next player has to play a deuce or pick up two more cards. If the next player can play another deuce, the player after them has to pick up four cards, unless they also have a deuce—and so it continues until a player can't put down a deuce and has to pick up two cards for every deuce put down.

**8**: The next player misses a turn.

**Jack back**: This card reverses the order of play.

**Last card rule**: If you have one card left in your hand, you must declare it before your turn has ended—if you forget, you have to pick up seven cards!

A hand organized according to suit and/or rank is easier to play.

There are several special cards that affect play—Aces, deuces, 8s, and Jacks.

## DEAL

Any player shuffles the cards and deals seven cards to each player, one at a time and face down. The remainder of the deck is placed face down in the middle to form the stock.

Players pick up their cards and sort them into suits.

## PLAY

The dealer flips over the top card of the stock to form a face-up pile and, so long as it isn't a special card, play begins. If it is a special card, the dealer turns over more cards from the stock until they find one that isn't. The player to the dealer's left plays a card that is either the same suit or rank and puts it on top of the face-up card. Players take it in turns and play moves clockwise around the table.

If a player can't put down a card or chooses not to for reasons of strategy, they draw one from the top of the stock pile.

If the stock pile runs out, the top card of the play pile is put to one side and the rest of the pile shuffled to form a new stock.

The winner is the first person to get rid of all their cards.

The play pile has been spread out to
show which cards have been played so far.
The player who put down A H chose
spades as the next suit.

# THIRTY-ONE

Also known as Blitz or Trente-et-un, there can be up to 15 players but the game works best with five or six. The aim is to get a value of 31 on cards in the same suit (a "blitz"), or three cards of the same rank.

### WHAT YOU NEED
- Standard deck of cards
- Jokers removed
- Five counters per player (such as buttons, coins, toothpicks)

### CARDS
Aces are high and count for 11, face cards 10, and others face value.

### ANTE
Each player puts one counter in the middle of the table (the "pot") before each deal.

### DEAL
Cut the cards to choose the dealer. The deal passes to the left after each round. The dealer shuffles and deals three cards, face down and one at a time, to each player, and another three cards face up in the middle of the table (the "widow"). The rest of the cards are put to one side and not used in the game.

Cards ranked from high to low.

**Widow**

Three cards are turned face up in the middle of the table to form the widow.

## PLAY

The player to the left of the dealer takes a card from the widow and replaces it with a card from their own hand. Each player in turn does the same. As soon as a player thinks they have the best possible hand, they knock. The other players can either "stand" with the cards they have or make one further exchange with the widow.

The player could swap Q C with 9 D in the widow and then knock, because 28 is a good score.

The player with the highest suit total wins the pot, unless beaten by three of a kind (known as "30½"). If there is a tie, players share the pot. If a player is out of counters, they are out of the game. The winner is the player left with counters.

The highest score is 31 in the same suit.

The next best score after 31 is three of a kind.

# TRASH

The goal here is to assemble a set of cards ranging from Ace to 10, which can include wild cards. Each time a player completes their set, they are dealt one less card in the following round, until one player is dealt one card. You can shorten the game to five or six rounds.

## WHAT YOU NEED

- Standard deck of cards
- Two decks if three or four players, three decks if five or six players

## CARDS

Jokers and Kings are wild and can go anywhere. If you later pick up a card where a wild card is sitting, you can swap them out.

Jacks and Queens don't count in this game and end a player's turn if they are turned up.

## DEAL

Any player shuffles the cards and deals ten cards to each player, face down and one at a time. The rest of the cards are placed in the middle of the table in a face-down pile to form the stock. The top card of the stock is flipped over and set beside the stock to form a discard pile.

Without looking at them, each player lines their cards up in two rows of five cards each, or one row of ten.

## PLAY

The player to the dealer's left takes a card from the stock or the discard pile and places it in the position in the row that matches the card. For example, an Ace goes in the top left spot, a 10 in the bottom right spot.

The player flips over the card that was already in that spot and places it in another spot if they can do so. A player's turn continues until they flip a card that cannot be placed, such as a Jack or a Queen, or a card they've already put down. That card goes on the discard pile and it's the next player's turn.

The first player to place all ten cards face up in a row shouts "Trash!" and ends the round. When this happens, all other players get to draw one more card to try to complete their set.

The winner of the last round shuffles the cards and starts the next. Anyone who had a full set last time is dealt nine cards, everyone else gets ten.

The game continues in this pattern until one player is dealt one card, which they have to replace with an Ace or wild card. If they succeed, they say "Trash!" to end the game.

Stock    Discard pile

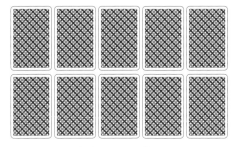

Each player's initial layout—
two rows of five cards.

Jokers and Kings are
wild cards.

Stock    Discard pile

Jacks and Queens end
a player's turn.

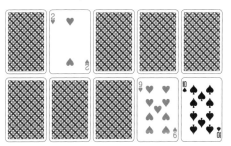

Game in progress—the Jack
has ended a player's turn.

# GAMES FOR AGES 12+

These are games for experienced players, and suitable for older children, teens, and adults. Skill, strategy, and a good memory for cards played are the keys to success here—though luck counts, too! There are some fancy words to learn that will make you feel like a professional when playing the games. Players will also learn how to bid, how to use trumps, and how to play in partnerships.

This trick-taking game is unusual in that the winner of the round is the player who wins the sixth and last trick. Everyone should agree beforehand how many rounds will be played to decide the winner of the game.

## WHAT YOU NEED
- Standard deck of cards
- Jokers removed

## CARDS
Strip out Kings, Queens, Jacks, deuces, and Ace of spades.

Aces are high, threes are low. The highest spade is the 10 of spades.

## DEAL
Any player deals six cards to each player, three at a time.

## PLAY
The player on the left of the dealer lays down a card. Play moves clockwise around the table, and the next player follows suit if possible. If they cannot do this, they may play any card they like. After every player has put down a card, the player who put down the highest card in the original suit wins the trick. That player now lays down a card to start the next trick and the game continues with play moving clockwise to the left.

The winner of the sixth trick wins the round. The deal passes to the left after each round.

Cards ranked from high to low.

10 D wins as the highest card of the original suit.

A more complicated but very popular version of Hearts (see page 52), this is also known as Black Lady and Rickety Kate, among other names. As well as all the hearts as penalty cards, the Queen of spades incurs an extra 13-point penalty for the player who's left with it in their hand. The British version of this game, Black Maria, has two extra penalty cards—the Ace and King of spades.

### WHAT YOU NEED

- Standard deck of cards
- Jokers removed
- Pencil and paper to keep score

### CARDS

Aces are high. Hearts and the Queen of spades are penalty cards. So that cards can be distributed evenly, if there are three players, remove the deuce of diamonds. If there are five players, remove the deuce of diamonds and deuce of clubs; if six players, remove all the deuces; if seven players, remove the deuce of diamonds, clubs, and spades.

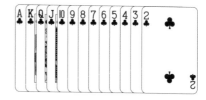

**HIGH**                                    **LOW**

Ranking of cards from high to low—
Ace is highest.

•  •  •  •  •  •  •  •  •  •  •  •  •  •  •  •  •  •  •  •  •
Instructions continue on next page
➡
•  •  •  •  •  •  •  •  •  •  •  •  •  •  •  •  •  •  •  •  •

Remove enough deuces to make
the deal come out even.

In the British version, known as Black Maria, the Ace of spades incurs 7 extra penalty points and the King of spades 10 points.

## DEAL

Cut the cards to see who deals first. The deal passes to the left after each round. The dealer shuffles the deck and deals out all the cards, one at a time and face down.

## PLAY

Players look at their cards and pass three cards they don't want face down to the player on their left while at the same time receiving three cards from the player on their right. They must not look at the cards they have received until they have passed on their discards.

The player to the left of the dealer starts the game by laying down the first card. Other players must follow suit; if a player does not have a card in that suit they may put down any other card.

The highest card of the suit that was first laid down wins the trick. The winner places it face down in front of them and starts the next trick. Play continues until all cards are played.

## SCORING

Each hearts card captured incurs a penalty point, and there are 13 penalty points for the Queen of spades. The winner is the player who has the lowest score when a target point is reached, or after a certain number of rounds.

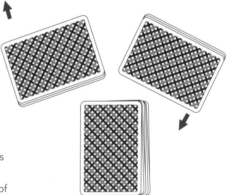

Players pass three cards to the player on the right and receive three cards from the player on their left.

## SHOOTING THE MOON

If a player has a bad hand and lots of hearts, they can try to "shoot the moon"—capture all the hearts and the Queen of spades. If they do this, they subtract 26 points from their score, or everyone else gets 26 points and they score 0.

The highest card is A C and wins the trick.

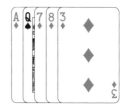

Player 2 has no diamonds so is able to discard the Queen of spades (player 1 wins the trick).

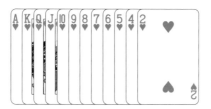

All hearts count for one penalty point per card. The player left with the Queen of spades racks up an extra 13 penalty points.

# BLACKJACK

In this popular gambling game, also known as Pontoon, Twenty-one, or Vingt-et-un, each player competes against the banker rather than each other. The aim is to get as close to 21 as possible without going over, and to have a better hand than the banker's. A game played at home is different to the casino version, and here the rules have been simplified to make it easier to play.

## WHAT YOU NEED
- Standard deck of cards
- Jokers removed
- At least 20 counters or tokens per player to use as stakes—agree beforehand what the minimum and maximum stake will be (say, a minimum of one and a maximum of three)

## CARDS
Aces count as 1 or 11. All face cards are worth 10; other cards take their face value.

## BEFORE YOU BEGIN
Cut the cards to choose who becomes banker first. Now decide how the deal will be transferred to the next person—this could be after six rounds, say, or after another player gets a blackjack (an Ace and a 10 or face card).

## DEAL
Banker shuffles the cards before the first deal but not thereafter—the cards are only reshuffled when the next player becomes banker. The banker deals one card face down to each player, dealer's last.

## FIRST CARD
All players except the banker look at their cards and place a stake (bet) in front of them, based on what they think their next card might be. The best possible hand is a two-card 21 or a five-card trick (five cards that total less or equal to 21). So if you had an Ace or a 10, for example, your chances are good. If you have a 6, make the lowest bet possible as this is the worst card. The banker then deals another card face down to each player.

## PLAY
Players look at their cards again. They choose one of the following moves:
**Blackjack**: If a player's first two cards are an Ace and a 10 card (a 10 or a face card), they have Blackjack, or a "natural" (also known as "pontoon").

The player turns the Ace face up on top of the other card and the turn passes to the next player.

**Stand:** If a player has cards with a total of 16 or more, they can stand (also known as "stick" or "stay") and no more cards will be dealt to them.

**Hit (twist):** A player can ask the banker for up to three cards, one at a time, which are dealt face up.

**Split:** If a player's first two cards are the same, they can treat them as two

Instructions continue on next page ➡

Ace counts for 1 or 11.

Face cards are worth 10 each.

An Ace and any face card equals a Blackjack—you don't have to have a Jack of clubs or spades.

The player has 13 points so should ask the banker for more cards, saying "Hit me!"

The player has 17 points so should stand, because they are likely to go bust with another card.

Bust

Banker

Winner

The banker must pay the winner the amount
equal to the winner's bet.

separate hands when it's their turn to play. They turn both cards face up and place a stake on each card. The banker deals one more card face down on each of these cards, and both hands can then be played as normal.

When receiving extra cards from the banker, if at any point the value of the cards exceeds 21 the player must turn their cards over and go bust. At this point their cards are added to the bottom of the deck and the banker takes the player's stake.

The banker now turns over their cards and either stands or hits until they have finished their turn. All other players then turn over their cards and the banker pays out to those who have won and collects the stakes of those who have lost. If the banker deals themselves a card that takes them over 21, they have gone bust and they must pay all the other players as follows:

- an amount equal to the player's original stakes
- double in the case of a Blackjack or five-card trick
- triple in the case of three sevens.

## WINNING THE GAME

The winning hand is that which is closest to 21. If a player ties with a banker, the banker wins. If a player ties with another player, two new cards are dealt to each and the person with the highest sum of those two cards wins.

The best hands in Blackjack—Blackjack, five-card trick, and three sevens.

# CALIFORNIA JACK

Also known as Callie Jacks, this is a two-player trick-taking game where the aim is to reach 10 points before your opponent by winning specific cards. The scoring system is a little tricky (see below) but it's what makes it such an interesting game. To make it easier, focus on getting the Ace, deuce, and Jack of trumps, and the highest number of tricks rather than Game (having the cards with the highest total in your tricks).

### WHAT YOU NEED
- Standard deck of cards
- Jokers removed
- Pencil and paper to keep score

### CARDS
Ace high, deuce low in all suits including trumps.

### DEAL
Cut the cards to see who deals first. Players take it in turns to deal. The dealer deals six cards to each player, face down and three at a time. The remaining cards are placed in a neat pile in the center of the table to form the stock pile. The dealer flips over the top card and this sets the trump suit for the round.

### PLAY
The player who didn't deal puts down any card. The second player must follow suit if possible. The winner of the trick is the player who puts down the highest card in the original suit or a trump.

The dealer turns over the top card to set the trump suit—here, clubs.

Player 1 wins the trick with the highest card in the suit that was played first.

Player 2 wins the trick with a trump card.

When a player wins a trick they take the face-up card from the stock and add it to their hand.

The trick is put to one side. The loser takes the next face-down card from the stock and adds it to their hand.

Players only try to win the trick if they think the hidden card will be worse than the exposed one.

The winner of the last trick turns over the next card from the stock, but this time it doesn't change the trump suit.

Play continues with the winner of the last trick starting the next trick. The winner of this trick takes the face-up card, the other player takes another face-down card from the stock, and

play continues. When the stock is empty, the last six cards in the players' hands are played.

## SCORING

One point for each trick that contains High (Ace of trumps), Low (deuce of trumps), Jack of trumps, and Game (having the cards with the highest total in your pile of tricks, where 10 for each 10, 4 for Aces, 3 for Kings, 2 for Queens, and 1 for Jacks). If Game is too tricky to calculate, just give 1 point to the winner of the most tricks.

The first player to score 10 points wins the game. If both players reach 10 in the same round, the points count in order (High, Low, Jack, Game).

Neither player wants to win this trick so they both play low cards and no trumps.

Players score 1 point for Ace, deuce, and Jack of trumps.

Players score 10 for each 10, 4 for Aces, 3 for Kings, 2 for Queens, and 1 for Jacks—the player with the highest total then gets 1 point for Game.

# CATCH THE TEN

Also known as Scotch Whist (although it's not like Whist at all), the goal is to win as many tricks as possible, especially those with the top trumps. You can play in partnerships if there is an even number of players, in which case partners should sit across from each other.

### WHAT YOU NEED
- Standard deck of cards
- Jokers and deuces, 3s, 4s, and 5s removed
- Pencil and paper to keep score

### CARDS
Normally 36 cards, ranking from Ace high to six low. The Jack ranks highest when in the trump suit. Remove the 6 of spades if there are five or seven players; add all the 5s if there are eight players.

### DEAL
Cut the cards to see who deals first. The dealer shuffles the cards and deals the cards face down and one at a time according to the number of players. So, nine cards are dealt to four players,

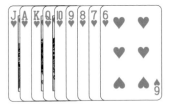

Ranking of cards from high to low—
Ace is highest.

If there are five or seven players,
remove 6 S before dealing.

Ranking of cards in trump suit—
Jack is highest.

Add all the 5s if there
are eight players.

seven to five players, six to six players, five to seven players, and five cards to eight players.

If there are two players, deal three separate hands of six cards each; if there are three players, deal two separate hands of nine cards each.

Each hand is then played separately with the cards not being looked at until the previous hand is played out.

The dealer's last card is always turned up to establish the trump suit. The dealer adds this card to their hand and can now play any card to the first trick.

**PLAYER 1**

Instructions continue on next page ➡

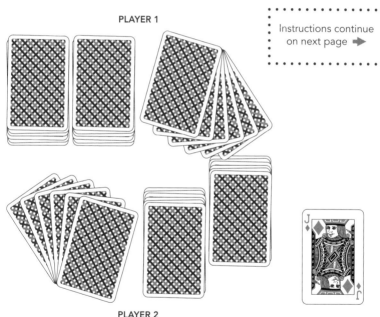

**PLAYER 2**

If there are two players, they will be dealt three hands of six cards each. Three players will have two hands of nine cards each, and each hand will be played separately.

Dealer's last card sets the trump suit.

## PLAY

The player to the left of the dealer plays any card from their hand. Play continues clockwise with players following suit, laying down a trump, or discarding a card. The trick is won by the highest card in the suit or by the highest trump. The player who wins the trick puts it by their side and starts the next one. Play continues until all cards have been played.

In this sample trick, every player has been able to follow suit and the Queen wins (put down by player 2).

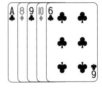

In this sample trick, diamonds are trumps and player 4 has won.

## SCORING

At the end of the round, points are awarded for the number of high trumps as follows: 11 points for the Jack, 10 for the 10, 4 for the Ace, 3 for the King, 2 for the Queen. Lower scoring trumps do not get any points. Each player also adds 1 point for every card captured in excess of the number originally dealt. For example, if four people play, a player who starts off with nine cards and wins four tricks (ending up with 12 cards) scores 3 extra points. The game ends when a player or partnership reaches an agreed number of points, usually 41. If two or more partnerships or players reach 41 at the end of a hand, calculate the score in the order of trumps to see who reached 41 first.

Points are awarded for tricks won with high-scoring trumps.

# GERMAN WHIST

This is a two-player Whist game (see page 122) with the deal alternating after each hand. The play is in two stages: the first is where players compete to win good cards from the stock and the second is where they compete to win the most tricks.

## WHAT YOU NEED

- Standard deck of cards
- Jokers removed

## CARDS

Aces are high.

## DEAL

Cut the cards to decide who deals. The dealer deals 13 cards to each player, face down. The remainder of the cards are placed face down in the middle of the table to form the stock. The dealer turns over the top card of the stock and places it on top of the pile. The suit of this card determines the trump cards for the whole of the hand.

## FIRST STAGE

The nondealer lays down the first card in the trick. They can put down any card, and their opponent should follow suit if they can, or play any other card. The winner is the highest card in the suit or a trump card, but in this stage you only try to win the trick if you think the card under the face-up one will be worse than the exposed one. For example, if

Dealer

Instructions continue on next page ➡

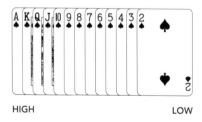

HIGH                                    LOW

Cards ranked from high to low.

Opponent

The dealer turns over the top card to set the trump suit.

# GERMAN WHIST CONTINUED

diamonds are trumps and the face-up card is a 6 of spades, the hidden card is likely to be better.

When a player wins a trick they take the face-up card from the stock and add it to their hand. The trick is put to one side and discarded. The loser takes the next face-down card from the stock and adds it to their hand so both players still have 13 cards.

The winner of the last trick turns over the next card from the stock, but this time it doesn't change the trump suit.

Play continues with the winner of the last trick leading with a card in the new trick. The winner of this trick takes the face-up card, the other player another face-down card, and play continues until the stock is empty.

## SECOND STAGE

The winner of the last trick in the first stage (the 13th trick) puts down the next card, and play continues for another 13 tricks until both players run out of cards. Trumps are the same as they were in the first stage. In the second stage, the players keep the

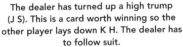

The dealer has turned up a high trump (J S). This is a card worth winning so the other player lays down K H. The dealer has to follow suit.

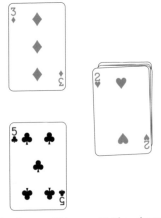

Spades are still trumps. Neither player wants to win this card so they both try to lose the trick by playing low cards.

tricks they have won and count them up at the end of the stage.

The winner is the player with the most tricks won in the second stage.

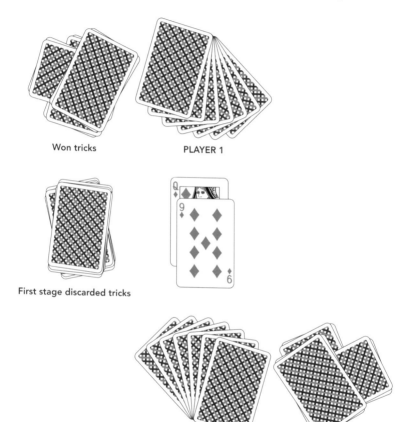

Won tricks

PLAYER 1

First stage discarded tricks

PLAYER 2

Won tricks

In the second stage, players keep the tricks they win and count them up at the end.

# JACKS

A game for three players, rather like Whist (see page 122), but where Jacks, or Knaves, are penalty cards. The object is to avoid winning tricks with Jacks, so it's what's called a "nullo game," like Hearts (see page 52) and American Hearts (see page 93).

## WHAT YOU NEED
- Standard deck of cards
- Jokers removed
- Pencil and paper to keep score

## CARDS
Aces are high, deuces are low. Each trick is a group of three cards. Trump cards outrank any other from a plain suit.

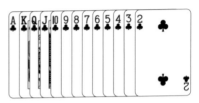

HIGH                                                          LOW

Ranking of cards from high to low—
Ace is highest.

## DEAL
Cut the cards to see who deals first. Subsequent deals pass clockwise to the left. The dealer deals out 17 cards to each player, face down and one at a time. The last card is turned face up on the table to determine the trump suit and is then set to one side.

The last card decides the trump suit.

## PLAY
The player to the dealer's left puts down any card face up on the table. Going clockwise around the table, each player takes it in turn to follow suit, if they can. If they can't, they may put down a trump card or any other card.

The King of diamonds wins as the highest card in the lead suit.

The trick is won by the person who plays the highest card in the leading suit or the highest trump card.

The winner takes the trick and places it face down in front of them.

## STRATEGY

Each person plays for themselves but if one player was way in the lead, the other two could form a temporary partnership to prevent that player from winning more tricks and forcing them to win tricks that contain Jacks.

## SCORING

Each trick won is worth 1 point, so there are 17 trick points to be won. There are 10 minus points for the Jacks—4 for the Jack of hearts, 3 for the Jack of diamonds, 2 for the Jack of clubs, and 1 for the Jack of spades. The winner is the first person to score 20 points.

This player has many trumps, so it looks like a good hand. However, although this means they can win many tricks, they are also likely to be forced to take Jacks.

This player only has a high spade to follow suit, so the next player has managed to get rid of a Jack.

4 penalty points

3 penalty points

2 penalty points

1 penalty point

# KNOCKOUT WHIST

Also known as Rat and Trumps, there are a maximum of seven deals, with a card fewer each time. The aim is to win tricks to avoid being knocked out, and to be the last player left in the game.

## WHAT YOU NEED
- Standard deck of cards
- Jokers removed

## CARDS
Aces are high. Trump suits change with each deal.

Each trick is a group of cards, one from each player. Trumps are special cards that outrank any other from a plain suit.

## DEAL
Cut the cards to see who deals first. Subsequent deals pass clockwise.

There are several deals in a game, and in each new deal players have one less card in their hands. In the first deal, seven cards are dealt face down and one at a time to each player. The rest of the deck is placed face down in a neat pile on the table and the top card turned over to establish trumps. In subsequent rounds, the winner of the last round chooses the trump suit after looking at their hand.

## PLAY
The player to the dealer's left leads by putting down any card face up on the

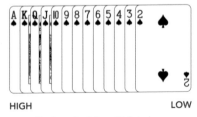

HIGH          LOW

Cards ranked from high to low.

table. Going clockwise around the table, each player takes it in turn to follow suit, if they can. If they can't, they may put down a trump card or any other card. The trick is won by the person who plays the highest card in the leading suit or the highest trump card.

If a person fails to win any tricks they are out of the game—unless they are the first player to take no tricks, in which case they can have a Dog's Life (see right). Play continues until all seven tricks have been played. The deal passes to the left and the person who won the most tricks begins the next round—if there is a tie, players cut the cards to decide who calls trumps and leads the first trick of the next round.

## DOG'S LIFE

The first player who fails to win any tricks is dealt one card in the next round, which they can play during any trick to reenter the game. If they don't win a trick this time, they're out of the game. If they do win a trick, they are dealt the same amount of cards as the other players in the next round.

The winner of the final trick in the last hand wins the game—or wins by being the last person standing if all the others have been knocked out.

| Trump suit | Highest card in suit first played wins | Trump wins |
|---|---|---|

Two examples of four-player tricks, with spades as trumps.

A player who was the first to be knocked out is dealt one card for a chance to reenter the game.

# OH HELL

Other names for this very popular game include Oh Well, Pshaw, Blackout, Blob, Elevator, and Contract Whist. Players try to predict the exact number of tricks they will win, no more, and no fewer. The game consists of a series of deals, each successive deal played with one more card.

## WHAT YOU NEED
- Standard deck of cards
- Jokers removed
- Pencil and paper to keep score

## CARDS
Aces are high.

## TRUMPS
The top card on the stock is turned up for trumps after each deal. When there is no stock (in the last deal of the game) there are no trumps—the highest card in the suit played first wins.

## DEAL
Cut the cards to see who deals first. Subsequent deals pass clockwise. There are several deals in a game. In the first deal, one card is dealt face down to each player; in the second deal, two cards; in the third, three; and so on, until no more deals are possible. This will vary according to the number of players—if there are five players, there will be ten deals, if four players, 13 deals.

Cards ranked—Ace is high.

The top card of the stock is turned over to set the trump suit—here, diamonds.

## BID

Players look at their cards and announce how many tricks they think they can win—for example, one or none in the first deal; two, one, or none in the second deal; and so on. The dealer makes a note of all the bids.

## HOW TO MAKE AN ACCURATE BID

With trumps, value the Ace and face cards as one trick each. Count all other Aces as one trick each, Kings as two-thirds of a trick, and Queens as half. However, if you have a lot of cards in a side suit (a suit that isn't trumps) take off a trick for each King and Ace, because you are at risk of being trumped.

In the third deal, if diamonds are trumps, this player has two high trump cards so should bid two tricks.

## PLAY

The player to the dealer's left leads by putting down their card face up on the table. Since players only have one card in the first deal, they have no choice about which card to play. The winner is the person who puts down the highest card in the suit played first or who trumped it.

The deal moves to the left of the first dealer, who shuffles the deck and deals each player two cards. The player who won the last trick chooses the trump suit and puts down the first card of the new trick.

Play continues in this way, with the number of cards dealt increasing with each deal, until all of the cards have been played.

## SCORING

The dealer writes down the score after every round. Players who fulfill their bids exactly win 1 point per trick plus an extra 10 points. If a player exceeds their bid they score nothing; they also score nothing if they fail to reach their bid.

The player with the highest score after all deals is the winner.

# POKER: FIVE-CARD DRAW

One of the two most popular forms of poker, along with Texas Hold'em (see page 118), this is a game of chance but also psychology. To make things more interesting, players place bets—and there's skill involved in correctly guessing whether another player is bluffing to win the pot, or whether they really do have the highest hand.

## WHAT YOU NEED

- Standard deck of cards
- Poker chips (or equivalent) for placing bets

## CARDS

To play poker, you need to be familiar with the hand rankings from highest to lowest so that you know whether your set of five cards is good or bad. The rankings are:

**1 Royal flush**: five consecutive cards, all in the same suit, from 10 to ace (highest hand).

**2 Straight flush**: any five consecutive cards in the same suit.

**3 Four of a kind**: four cards of the same rank in the four suits.

**4 Full house**: three cards of the same rank (three of a kind), plus two of the same rank.

**5 Flush**: five cards from the same suit but in no particular order.

**6 Straight**: five consecutive cards, but not from the same suit. Ace ranks low or high.

**7 Three of a kind**: three cards of the same rank.

**8 Two pair**: two sets of two cards of the same rank.

**9 One pair**: one set of two cards of the same rank.

**10 High card** (lowest hand).

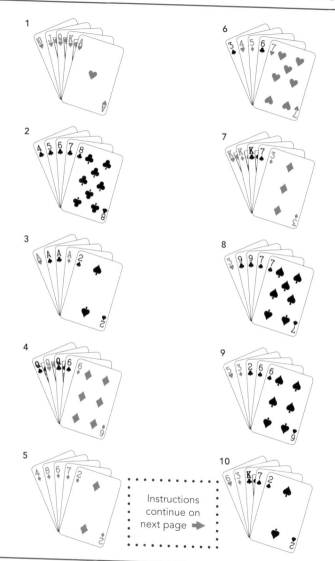

Instructions continue on next page ➡

## BETTING

Poker is a gambling game, and players usually bet with chips or money. If you decide to play for cash, it's best to set a limit on the amount that can be staked.

## DEAL

At the start of the game, every player must put down an initial amount of chips or money (the ante). The point of the ante is to stop players from immediately folding if they get a bad hand and forfeiting their initial bet. All the players are then dealt five cards face down by the dealer, starting with the player to the dealer's left. The rest of the deck is placed face down, ready to be dealt from.

## PLAY

The player to the left of the dealer goes first. They can either **check** (not bet anything) or place a bet. The next player can then **call** (match the previous player's bet), **raise** (match the previous player's bet and add a further amount), or **fold** (drop out of the hand, losing the chance of winning the pot). The next player does the same, until all players have either bet the same amount or folded. Any player who folds should leave their cards face down on the table so they can't be seen.

After this, the remaining players can discard up to three cards and take the same number of cards from the deck, in an attempt to improve their hand.

Now there's another round of betting, just like the first. Once all the players have either added the same amount of bets to the pot or folded, everyone reveals their cards. The player with the highest hand wins the pot.

## TACTICS

By watching what the other players are doing, such as how many cards they're discarding or how big their bets are, you can make guesses about what kind of hand they might have. Of course, the beauty of poker is that a skilled player can also bluff, appearing more confident to hide the fact that they actually have a weak hand. Alternatively, they might play cautiously to trick other players into thinking that their hand is weaker than it is.

The aim of the game is to win more hands than any other player by weighing up when it's best to call, raise, or fold.

**PLAYER 1**

After the deal, Player 1 has a good hand: three jacks, one 7, and one 8. They think they might be able to make a full house or four of a kind. They decide to raise, adding a further bet to the pot.

**PLAYER 2**

Player 2's hand is poor: nothing except a pair. Seeing Player 1's confidence, they decide to fold.

**PLAYER 3**

Player 3 has three consecutive cards from the same suit. With a bit of luck, they might be able to get a straight flush—or failing that, a flush. They decide to call, matching Player 1's bet.

After discarding one card for a new one from the deck, Player 1 ends up with a full house: three jacks and two sevens. He raises, adding more money to the pot.

Player 3 discards two cards and picks up two new ones. They're in luck—they have a straight flush. Player 3 raises again, so that Player 1 has to match their bet to stay in the game.

Now it's time to reveal their cards. Player 3 has the higher-ranking hand—a straight flush—so they win the pot.

# POKER: TEXAS HOLD'EM

Another popular—and slightly more complicated—poker variation, Texas Hold'em has players using their own two cards and a set of five community cards to try to build the highest hand and win the pot. The ranking system for hands is the same as in Five-Card Draw (see page 114).

## WHAT YOU NEED
- Standard deck of cards
- Poker chips (or equivalent) for placing bets

## DEAL

Cut the cards to see who deals first. The game starts with the dealer dealing two cards (hole cards) face down to each player from the top of the deck, starting with the player to the dealer's left.

## GAME

After every player has been dealt their two hole cards, there is a round of betting. This is the same as in five-card draw: every player takes it in turn to call, raise, or fold until all players have either added the same amount to the pot or folded and left the game.

Now the dealer turns over three cards (the **flop**) from the top of the deck and places them in the middle of the board so all the players can see them.

These are the community cards. The remaining players make their second bets based on how good a hand they think they can make from their two hole cards, the three community cards on the board, and the two more community cards still to be dealt.

After this round of betting has finished and all the players have either bet the same amount or folded, the dealer takes another card face up (the **turn**) from the deck. After this, the third round of betting takes place.

Once this round of betting is over, the dealer lays the fifth and final community card (the **river**). A fourth and final round of betting follows.

Now it's time for the showdown: the remaining players play the best hand that they can, using their two hole cards and the five community cards. The player with the highest hand wins the pot.

Community cards

**PLAYER 1**

Player 1 has five of hearts and seven of spades.

**PLAYER 2**

Player 2 has queen of diamonds and a two of clubs.

**PLAYER 3**

Player 3 has a nine of diamonds and a nine of hearts.

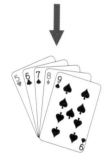

Player 1 uses their two hole cards to make a straight with the six, eight, and nine community cards.

Player 2 uses one of their hole cards to make a pair with the queen community card.

Player 3 uses both of their hole cards to make four of a kind with the two nines on the board.

Player 3 wins the pot.

# SPADES

In this game, spades are always trumps. It can be played either solo ("cutthroat") or as a partnership, where players work in teams and sit opposite each other. The aim is to be the first player or team to score a certain number of points—for example, 300.

## WHAT YOU NEED
- Standard deck of cards
- Jokers removed
- Pencil and paper to keep score

## CARDS
Aces are high. Spades are always trumps.

## DEAL
Cut the cards to see who deals first. Subsequent deals pass clockwise. The dealer deals out all the cards, face down and one at a time, so that each player has 13 cards.

## BID
Players look at their cards and arrange them into suits. Each player announces how many tricks they think they can win—the minimum bid is one. If playing in partnerships, each team adds together the two players' bids for the number of tricks they are chasing. The dealer makes a note of the bids and play begins.

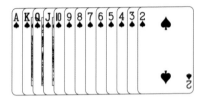

Cards ranked from high to low—spades are always trumps in this game.

## HOW TO MAKE AN ACCURATE BID
With trumps, value the Ace and face cards as one trick each. Count all other Aces as one trick each, Kings as two-thirds of a trick, and Queens as half. However, if you have a lot of cards in a side suit—a suit that isn't spades—consider taking off half a trick for each King and Ace, because you are at risk of being trumped.

The player to the dealer's left leads by putting down any card face up on the table. Going clockwise around the table, each player takes it in turn to follow suit. If they can't follow suit, they may put down a trump card or any other card.

The trick is won by the person who plays the highest card in the leading suit or the highest trump card.

The winner takes the trick and places it in front of them, face down. Each trick won is placed crosswise to make it easier to count up the number of tricks at the end of the round. The winner of the trick leads the next one, and the round continues until all 13 tricks have been played.

Spades cannot be the first card played until a trick has been trumped earlier in the round.

## SCORING

Players (or teams) who fulfill their bids exactly score 10 points per each trick bid, plus 1 "sandbag" for each extra trick ("overtrick"). For example, if a bid was four tricks and six were won, the score would be 40 points for the bid and 2 sandbags for the overtricks. The overtricks are noted separately and when 10 sandbags have been accumulated, the player or team loses 100 points—this is to encourage accurate bidding!

If a player or team fails to reach their bid they lose 10 points for each trick bid.

The first player or team to reach the target score wins the game.

A player has three face card trumps so should bid to win three tricks.

This player only has one low trump, which they might not be able to win with, and a long side suit, so a safe bid is one for the Ace of clubs.

# WHIST

This is a partnership game where players are seated opposite each other and cooperate to win as many tricks as possible. A popular and very enjoyable family game, Whist is easy to play, but more difficult to play well, although there are various strategies that will help. Competitive players will remember which high cards have been played and which ones are still out there waiting to take tricks.

## WHAT YOU NEED
- Standard deck of cards
- Jokers removed
- Pencil and paper to keep score

## CARDS
Aces are high. Each trick is a group of four cards. Trumps are special cards that outrank any other from a plain suit.

## DEAL
Cut the cards to see who deals first. Subsequent deals pass clockwise to the left.

The dealer deals all the cards, one at a time and face down. The dealer's final card is turned over and this sets the trumps for the round. The dealer then adds this card to their hand.

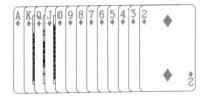

Cards ranked from high to low.

The dealer's final card is turned over to set the trump suit (in this example, clubs). Trump cards beat cards from any other suit.

## PLAY

The player to the dealer's left leads by putting down any card face up on the table. Going clockwise around the table, each player takes it in turn to follow suit, if they can. If they can't, then they may put down a trump card or any other card.

The trick is won by the person who plays the highest card in the leading suit or the highest trump card.

The winner takes the trick and places it in front of them, face down. Each trick won is placed crosswise to make it easier to count up the number of tricks at the end of the round.

## REVOKING

If a player "revokes" by not playing a card when they can, 2 points are given to the opposing partnership.

Play continues until all 13 tricks have been played. If a partnership wins all 13 tricks, this is called a "grand slam."

Instructions continue on next page ➡

Ace of hearts wins as the highest card in the suit first played.

The last card played wins the trick as it is a trump card.

Place tricks crosswise so each group of cards is separate and easier to count up.

## STRATEGY

The following details some strategies that are useful when playing Whist.

### LEAD CARD

The lead (first-played) card in the first trick dictates the play, and the player has the advantage of being able to communicate information to their partner about the state of their hand. Good options are:

- a low card from a suit of four or more cards (a long suit)— sometimes you can force your opponents to use up their trump cards prematurely to take the trick.

- a singleton—if you only have one card in a suit, it's good to lead with this because next time this suit turns up, you can trump it.

- a trump card—if you have five or more trump cards, you can reduce the number of your opponents' trump cards.

### PLAYING SECOND TO A TRICK

Play a low card in the hope that your partner can play a better one!

In general, except when trying to win a trick, you should always play the lowest card you can of the suit led. But if you only have two cards in that suit, play the highest and then the lowest to let your partner know that you can trump that suit if it comes up again, as you won't have any cards left in it.

In this sample hand, trumps are clubs. A good lead card to play is either J D (a singleton), because next time diamonds are led you can play a trump card, or 2 C to force your opponents to waste their trump cards.

Player 2 has put down a low card and their partner (player 4) was able to play a high card and win the trick.

## SCORING

**Tricks**: 1 point for each trick won above six in the round.

**Honors**: points are awarded to players who were dealt "honors"—Ace, King, Queen, and Jack of trumps. If one partnership were dealt four honors, they score 4 points. If three, they score 2 points. If each partnership has two honors, they don't count. Remember: honors go to those who were dealt them, not those who won them, so both teams may get points in the same deal—one for tricks, one for honors.

**Partnerships score points for honor cards they were dealt.**

The first team to reach 7 points (5 points in the British version) wins the game.

Tricks are scored before honors, and honor points can never be used for the last point to win a game.

Three games make a rubber. If the first two games are won by the same partnership, the third game is not played.

# GLOSSARY

**Bid** A declaration of how many tricks or points a player will win during a round.

**Cut** Lift a random number of cards from the top of the deck.

**Cutthroat** A game where everyone plays for themselves.

**Deal** Pass out cards to each player after shuffling the deck.

**Deuce** A 2 of any suit.

**Discard** Get rid of an unwanted card(s).

**Draw** Collect one or more cards from the stock.

**Exchange** Replace unwanted cards with new ones.

**Face cards** Jacks, Queens, and Kings (picture or court cards).

**Follow suit** Play a card that is the same suit as the lead card.

**Foundation (or base)** In solitaire-type games, where a player builds cards on a specific starting card (usually an Ace)

through the remaining ranks, either of the same suit or alternating between red and black cards.

**Hand** The cards a player holds in a game.

**Hole card** Cards in poker that are dealt face down so only the player can see them (also known as pocket or down cards).

**Lay off** To add a card to another player's meld.

**Lead** The first card put down.

**Long suit** Where a player holds more than the average number of cards in one suit.

**Meld** To match three or four cards of a kind or in sequence in the same suit.

**Natural** A card that isn't wild.

**Nullo game** Where players try to avoid taking certain cards.

**Order** The order in which cards are dealt, in which the participants take turns to play, and in which the deal passes from person to person is to the left (clockwise).

**Rank**  The value of each card relative to other cards.

**Round**  A phase of play in which every player has a chance to play.

**Shuffle**  Mix up the order of the cards in a deck before they are dealt.

**Side (plain) suit**  A suit that isn't trumps.

**Spot (or pip) cards**  All the cards except the Aces and face cards.

**Stock**  The undealt portion of the deck from which a player can draw new cards during play.

**Suits**  Groupings of cards—hearts, spades, diamonds, and clubs.

**Tableau**  The layout of the cards on the table.

**Trick**  A set of cards consisting of one card from each player in a round.

**Trump**  A suit of cards that outranks all the other cards in the deck.

**Upcard**  The top card of the stock, which is turned face up to start the discard pile.

**Widow**  An extra hand whose cards may be substituted for a player's own cards.

**Wild card**  A card that can represent any card.

This edition first published 2024 by Ammonite Press
An imprint of GMC Publications Ltd
Castle Place, 166 High Street, Lewes, East Sussex, BN7 1XU, United Kingdom

This title has been created with materials first published in *Cards Games* (2021)

ISBN 978-1-78145-491-6

A catalog record for this book is available from the British Library.

Publisher  Jonathan Bailey
Production Manager  Jim Bulley
Editor  Jane Roe
Designer  Robin Shields
Additional material  Nick Pierce

Set in Avenir
Color origination by GMC Reprographics
Printed in China

FSC

MIX

Paper

FSC® C144853

AMMONITE
PRESS

www.ammonitepress.com